THE CONVERSION EQUATION

THE
CONVERSION
EQUATION

A Proven Formula To Attract High-Level
Prospects, Close More Sales, And
Increase Your Profitability

Terri Levine, PhD

NEW YORK

LONDON • NASHVILLE • MELBOURNE • VANCOUVER

THE CONVERSION EQUATION
A Proven Formula To Attract High-Level Prospects, Close More Sales, And Increase Your Profitability

© 2021 Terri Levine, PhD

Published in New York, New York, by Morgan James Publishing. Morgan James is a trademark of Morgan James, LLC. www.MorganJamesPublishing.com

ISBN 978-1-63195-375-0 paperback
ISBN 978-1-63195-376-7 eBook
Library of Congress Control Number:

Morgan James is a proud partner of Habitat for Humanity Peninsula and Greater Williamsburg. Partners in building since 2006.

Get involved today! Visit
www.MorganJamesBuilds.com

DEDICATION

I know, you like me, pick up a book and go to the dedication, and don't see your name there.

Well, not this time!

If we haven't yet met, are acquaintances, are good friends, or if you are a client family member already, I wrote this book for YOU!

I care. You matter.

And so, I dedicate this book to YOU!

TABLE OF CONTENTS

CONVERSION EQUATION
SPECIAL MESSAGE

As a two-time Inc. 500 company founder, co-founder of a third company that reached nearly a $1B market value, and coach/advisor to leading off-and online businesses in over 300 industries, I have worked and collaborated with some of the top marketing experts and consultants in the world. Terri is one of those for small businesses.

As the father of "Business Growth Optimization and Maximization," for the last 20 years, my company has helped tens of thousands of businesses maximize lead generation, customer conversions, the lifetime value of these customers/ clients/patients—and turbo-charge their profitability and business value. In this book, Terri incorporates and builds upon these powerful business-building strategies and tools.

Helping entrepreneurial businesses achieve their goals requires the application of a success formula and proven system that produces consistent results. Terri has mastered such a system with the Conversion Equation.

I met Terri years ago when we were both speaking at a leading marketing event in Austin, Texas. We instantly bonded around our shared views for training and consulting entrepreneurial businesses. She is all about serving and helping her "family clients" produce real, tangible results—results that generate significant added revenue and profit while simultaneously creating life-changing freedom they desperately crave.

Terri has personally built 6 multi-million-dollar companies. She understands what it is like to deal with every aspect of starting and building a business. She has also helped 6,000 business owners in 400+ industries increase revenue and profit.

The Conversion Equation is an operator's manual that teaches you how to create and own the system for consistently generating high-quality leads, converting these into high-value transactions and then turning these customers into raving lifetime fans who will buy more from you over their customer life.

In this book, Terri methodically lays out her proven system, grounding the reader on the core principles all along the way. This book is jam-packed with practical actions you can immediately take to increase revenue and profit, both the short-and long-term.

Terri takes things to the next level by powerfully demonstrating how the strategies and tactics have worked with real-world client case studies throughout the book. You will quickly see how her blueprint system can help any business regardless of size, industry, marketing experience, or budget.

By the time you finish this book, Terri will have provided you with all the tools you need to put into practice what she teaches. This includes a template to help you create a 3-, 6-, or 12-month action plan to ensure you get your desired results.

Terri left nothing on the table. She provides the same information in this book as she does to paying clients where they guarantee to uncover at least $100,000.

I encourage you to read every chapter and every word because it just keeps building and building right up until the end.

—Scott Hallman
Two-time Inc. 500 company founder
#1 Amazon-Kindle Bestselling Author of
The 7 Success Drivers™ to HYPERGROWTH
Leading Business Growth and CEO Coach
HUGE Fan of Terri Levine's

FOREWORD

"One thousand prospects? Wow, that's a lot!" "Ummm ... Not actually."

I was teaching my friend about business and was sitting down doing math to help her understand how things actually work. What really matters. You know, the stuff they don't teach you in all of the rah-rah self-help business books.

I went on to explain to her that one thousand *qualified* prospects is a lot *in the right hands*. One thousand unqualified prospects in the wrong hands isn't much at all. Well, that's not quite right. It's a giant pain in the tuckus without any upside. If that's your thing, put this book down now.

What you hold in your hands will show you how to get qualified prospects into the right hands: *yours* if you pay attention to what Terri has to say about it.

I know for a fact that this type of marketing is what *really* works. I know this after 30 startups over the last 30 years—after coaching and consulting for thousands of businesses around the world —after writing books about marketing that now serve as university textbooks around the world.

After a while you begin to instantly recognize what will work and what won't. And you also begin to recognize which alleged "business gurus" out there know their stuff and which ones are merely parroting what they've heard others say.

Terri knows her stuff. This book is loaded with practical advice hard won in the trenches.

And if you don't think qualified prospects in the right hands is a big deal, think of it this way: it's the fastest legal way to hoard stockpiles of cash. The better you get at this stuff, the faster the stockpiles will grow.

If you get to work.

Will you? If so, read on. If not, don't torture yourself. Not everyone is cut out to be an entrepreneur.

All the best,

Mark Joyner

Founder and CEO

Simpleology-*Simplicity is freedom!*

www.simpleology.com

ACKNOWLEDGMENTS

First, I would like to thank Kathy Sparrow for her dedication to my book and her editing. I am also very grateful for Morgan James Publishing in supporting this book and bringing it to fruition.

I'd also like to thank all the people I have learned from as great mentors and consultants over the years including Joe Vitale, Scott Hallman, Jay Abraham, Joel Bauer, Karl Bryan, and Mark Joyner.

Additionally, my special thanks to Lee Constantine, Terry Whalin, Ellen Violette, Nasir Jamil, and Barbra Portzline. I could not have done this without your help and belief in my book.

An additional thanks to my client family members who enjoy my mentoring, consulting, teaching, and training, and allow me to help them apply the Conversion Equation in their businesses.

INTRODUCTION

Business owners today are frustrated and struggling to get leads, close sales, and create consistent income. The global economy is in shambles. Every day I speak with business owners who are not getting any return on investment with their advertising and marketing as these efforts just don't work as well anymore. I hear their frustrations, and I understand their struggles and challenges.

If you are also struggling, frustrated, and feeling challenged in this economy and with ineffective marketing, you have picked up the right book for sure! If you relate to this at all as a business owner or an entrepreneur, you must learn the material. As a business and marketing consultant and strategist for many decades, I have helped over 6,000 business owners, just like you. I will show you how to generate more leads, close more sales, and make more income, as we take a journey together with me as your guide. The Conversion Equation—and all the other information I share in this book are the solutions you have been searching for, hoping for, waiting for, and, perhaps, even praying for.

I understand you. I know you are desperate for proven and tested ways to generate more qualified leads, attract more clients, patients, or customers to your business and make more money. I will take you by the hand and guide you in this book, so you stop making marketing mistakes and have consistent success in your business. Embrace me as your business strategist right now, and I will show you the way.

CHAPTER 1
EVERYTHING YOU EVER LEARNED OR HEARD ABOUT MARKETING IS WRONG!

S uppose you want to know why you are struggling to have a consistent stream of highly qualified prospects who are excited to buy your products and services. In that case, the answer is you probably don't know how to do proven marketing that attracts customers to your business successfully.

As a business and marketing consultant and strategist, who created multi-million-dollar businesses in many different industries, I have has helped over 6,000 small business owners in 444 various industries worldwide. I have a proven formula to produce qualified prospects, and it will work in your business.

Before I teach this to you, I want you to know that you've been doing marketing wrong. I mean, all wrong. And this is certainly not your fault. In my experience, most business owners believe that if they create some type of attention-grabbing marketing, they will magically generate leads. Nothing could be further from the truth I will quickly show you that most businesses make three huge lead generation mistakes. And these mistakes can be corrected.

If you are a typical business, you try a marketing tactic and spend time and money, hoping it will be effective and bring you a return on investment. Maybe you have attempted things like Facebook ads, or pay-per-click ads, or off-line advertising, or you have been busy creating PowerPoints or starting Facebook groups. Like most business owners, your marketing results in very few prospects who have any interest in your offerings. You feel down because you put so much time and money into marketing, and you never get that time or money back. Ideally, you dream of having more money and getting real results from your marketing. You want to have more qualified prospects converting into paying customers. Does any of this sound like you? If so…

I will show you the exact system that brings my client family members' marketing results, making more money in less time and with less effort. These are the systems I use in my own business. We all spend little time marketing so we can focus on serving our paid customers.

The marketing system I will be showing you and helping you implement is systematic and will leverage your marketing and give you real results by changing the way you do all of your marketing and advertising forever.

There is nothing scary here. There are no big radical changes. Based on simple, common-sense changes, my system will exponentially leverage your marketing results. If you have been spending $10,000 on an ad and getting dismal results, you will see how to make an ad that will give you results that will pay off and will allow you to become the leader in your industry. If you have been spending time on social media with organic marketing with little to no results, that too, is about to change.

This system will allow you to make more money while you spend much less time and effort on marketing. Because most of your competitors do not know this system, you will have a real advantage in your marketing. Instead of hit-and-miss results that are unpredictable, you will have a lead generating marketing machine. Yes, a conveyor belt of qualified prospects.

As a clinical psychologist, I understand human behavior and the principles that guide people to respond to marketing and advertising and why and how they buy. I will take you behind the scenes, so you don't have to get a Ph.D. in marketing and have enough understanding of human behavior to make your marketing effective.

Marketing's Job

Marketing must help a prospect who is going to become one of your customers feel that they have made the best buying decision possible. Instead of talking endlessly or having long, convincing sales pages that go on and on, waxing eloquent about how amazing you and your company are and all your benefits, you will learn to do marketing that allows your buyers be in total control of their decision-making process. Once you have provided a qualified prospective buyer the right kinds of information, it will become clear to them that they are receiving the most value for the price they pay, and they will purchase your products and services.

Everything in my system is simple to understand and so easy to apply. I have thousands of client family member success stories in all kinds of businesses and industries. My proven system works for them, and it will work for you.

When you finish reading this book, you will have learned common-sense principles of marketing that you will be able to apply right away. You will know exactly how to do marketing and how not to do marketing.

Your marketing will crush your competition and give you a significant advantage over your competitors when you implement this system.

Let's get started.

Three Marketing Mistakes Revealed

The three major marketing mistakes I see with small business owners are so common and also very easily corrected—once you know how.

The first mistake is that business owners go it alone. They do not have a proven marketing formula and have not spent years studying and testing marketing. Yet, they do not get any professional help, and they keep trying different tactics and hoping something will stick. Or they get help from a self-proclaimed marketing "guru" or a course that doesn't work. Are you making any of these mistakes?

The second marketing mistake is that most entrepreneurs and business owners do not know the marketing fundamentals required to get qualified prospects, close prospects, and generate income. So, they keep trying things and spending money and time and energy on wasted sales and marketing that does not result in leads and income. Does this sound familiar?

Then, the third marketing mistake business owners make: they do not know what to do with their marketing, so it doesn't generate cash flow.

Be honest, are you making any of these mistakes?

Now it's time to explore these mistakes, and then I will help you easily and systematically overcome them.

But before we go on, take a moment to pause. I am curious: are you using any marketing strategies and tactics right now? Maybe you've produced an ad, brochure, postcard, flyer, website, webinar, podcast, or blog? Well, suppose that the marketing piece does not follow the lead generation secrets. In that case, I'm about to reveal to you that even most marketers and business strategists and consultants do not know, you probably won't get results. It is not your fault. You have not learned the Conversion Equation.

Once you adopt the Conversion Equation, you must also learn how to apply it correctly. When you do, you will no longer compete on price. You will have more qualified prospects, and your marketing and advertising effectiveness will typically increase more than 100 times. You will also convert more prospects and dramatically increase your sales.

I like to think of this system as a way to turn on—and tune in—your marketing faucet to always be able to control your marketing and turn up the flow whenever you want more prospects.

Getting in Control of Your Marketing

Business owners typically make the first mistake because they have no idea what marketing is supposed to do. Let me explain. The purpose of marketing is to capture the attention of your exact target market by relating to their "pain" or "problem." You'll then show them that you have a solution to remove their pain or problem and that you are the only business who can do that. The next step is to lower the risk of them engaging in the buying process while educating your qualified prospects regarding the value you offer.

When you market using the Conversion Equation and stop doing marketing wrong, you will have more prospects and customers deciding to do business with you. I mean this, regardless of price.

You may have heard that 96% of all small businesses fail within their first 5 years. In my experience, these business owners fail because they lack expertise in lead generation. Everything people are teaching about marketing is based on trying many different tactics and hoping something will work. Instead, marketing must be approached with a proven system based on strategy than tactics. When you do your marketing the right way, the lead generation problem is corrected, and your chances of having a successful and profitable business are significantly increased.

This distinction between strategic and tactical marketing is huge and is one that you need to be acutely aware of before I teach you about generating more leads. I go into much more detail later in the book. However, for now, understand that placing ads, sending out mailers, joining a networking group, attending tradeshows, implementing a prospecting follow-up system, and anything else you might currently be doing is simply a tactic.

You must understand the strategic side of marketing. Strategic marketing is what you say in your marketing and how you say it. Strategy is always more important than the marketing medium or tactic.

Failure to make this distinction means your marketing will most likely fail. If you wonder why your marketing has not worked for you in the past, it most likely is not the marketing medium's fault. Instead of blaming the tactic for failing and saying that email does not work, or Facebook ads do not work, you need to look at your strategic marketing message. That is where you are typically making big mistakes. If your marketing isn't getting you the results you want, this is either because of poor strategy or poor tactical execution.

If you are like most business owners, a major marketing mistake you are making is using many platitudes in your marketing. Platitudes are statements such as, "We have the lowest prices," "We provide the best quality, "We have great customer service," "We have been in business 29 years," "We have convenient parking," or "I am a bestselling author" There are many more but I'm sure by now you get the point.

Here's the moment of truth: Take a look at any of your current marketing. Is it filled with platitudes? I guess that it is. Small business owners have been taught to believe platitudes are the correct way to market their businesses. Why? Most advertising, including the Fortune 500 firms, do their marketing this way. Think about the ads you see on TV or in magazines or on-line. They are filled with platitudes. When everyone has this type of marketing, prospects will buy from the business that offers the lowest price since all the companies look the same.

Check your marketing messages. If your marketing is based on platitudes, you will forever need to compete on price, often devaluing your products and services.

Ok, now are you ready for the good news and how to generate all the qualified prospects your business can handle? I will give you a quick overview of the *Conversion Equation* right now.

Then we will go through this proven formula in great detail in the rest of the chapters so you can apply the formula and generate more leads, close more sales and make more income!

4 Components of the Conversion Equation

The Conversion Equation has 4 components that, when used together, transform your marketing endeavors and create the results you want—or perhaps desperately need.

Interrupt: To get a qualified prospect to pay attention to your lead generation, you must interrupt the prospect's attention with your written or verbal headline. This applies to ads, emails, websites, networking, podcasts, when speaking with prospects—everything. You will always begin by interrupting your prospects. You interrupt them with some type of verbal, written, video, or audio where your headlines grab their attention.

Engage: Once a prospect has been interrupted, you must show them in a sub-heading—again verbal, written, video, or audio—that you have a solution for their problem. This component is "engage." Once you have interrupted them with a problem, now you must quickly engage them with your resolution.

Educate: Next, you need to "educate" your prospect. You have to give your audience information that instantly shows how and why you solve the exact problem they are experiencing. You accomplish this by providing them with detailed, quantifiable, specific, and revealing information. Consider this the copy of your ad or the essence of a video that follows the headline and then the sub-headline.

Education shows them what information they need to know when buying a solution to their problem. You will demonstrate that ONLY your business has the solution they are seeking.

When you interrupt and engage, you must hit your prospects' emotional hot buttons, as well. Being transparent, this is not easy, so I will be showing you exactly how to do this in other chapters.

Offer: Finally, the last part of the Conversion Equation is to make an "offer." So, first, you *interrupt* a prospect with a problem, then you *engage* them with promising a solution to their problem, then you *educate* them, and show them how you help them solve their problem—and now you need to make them a low or no-risk way to take the next step in your sales process. The *offer* can be a checklist, template, video, audio, webinar, or anything else that will allow them to take the next step.

For example, I use this as my offer (www.tlwebinar.com): We have prospects watch a free, educational training. At the end of the training, if they want to consider doing business with us, we have another low risk (www.tlwebinar.com/blueprint) way solution.

Today, I rarely see people using this proven marketing formula. When I look at most marketing, it only uses one or two parts of the equation. Usually, the ad gets my attention; however, it does not engage me or educate me. Same with a business owners' website, their emails, their social media headers, etc.

Most marketing today is filled with jargon and slogans. Big businesses, like Nike or Coke, can afford to get us to hear their slogans. However, this strategy does not work in small business. As a small business owner, you don't have the huge marketing budgets these big brands have.

However, you don't need one when you use the Conversion Equation. Here is what can happen for you.

⑤ CASE STUDY—CHIROPRACTOR ⑤

One of my client family members, Dr. Joshua, was almost out of business. He was spending over $5,000 a month on Facebook ads with almost no results. He got one lead per month and was closing 1 person every 2 months. His business was about to go under.

I looked at his Facebook ads and realized instantly they did not follow the Conversion Equation. The ads were making offers that said "call us" as their call to action. There was no interrupt at all in the ads. The ads listed all the generic and "me too" services that every one of his competitors offers. These ads contained very generic and typical marketing messages about helping relieve back pain, migraines, injuries, etc.

Very quickly, I redesigned his Facebook ads. Instead of mentioning generic problems chiropractors address, we identified his patients' biggest problem when seeking his help. He told me he mostly saw men who were weekend warriors and who had injured their backs doing sports and had a lot of pain. That became the emotional hot button we wanted the ads to focus on.

Since all chiropractors work with back pain, he had to hit specifically why his business was different. We came up with something unique that his competitors did not claim. He had a 3-step process that guaranteed after only 7 chiropractic sessions, his patients could potentially eliminate back pain forever. Now, he could stand alone in his field. All we needed to do is take this information and apply it to the Conversion Equation.

The new Facebook ads interrupted his prospects. I made sure that the headline addressed the main hot button problems that his weekend warrior patients were looking to solve. In this case, back pain.

The headline, designed to *interrupt* his exact target market, said, "Most chiropractors insist you see them for long-term and never get rid of your weekend warrior back pain." Do you think his exact prospects might relate to this headline?

Next, the ads promised a solution to *engage* his prospects. The headline highlighted back pain and referenced that most chiropractors expect you to see them long-term. We engaged his prospects with his solution. In the sub-head, we said, "Ask any chiropractor these 3 questions to be sure you won't be one of their patients forever." When his prospects read the sub-headline, they became curious about what the three questions were.

Then, it was time to *educate* them. Readers were instructed to ask the chiropractors they were working with or considering going to:

- If they guaranteed to cure their back pain in only 7 sessions
- If they could not cure the pain in 7 sessions would they give them free sessions until the pain was cured, or
- Would they give them their money back?

He already knew the average chiropractor would not be willing or able to make these guarantees. This is where his Core Unique Positioning Statement* (CUPS), which I will teach you about in a later chapter, came in. His CUPS stated if he could not help them in 7 sessions their money would be cheerfully refunded, and he could stand behind this guarantee. This made his chiropractic service THE logical choice.

His offer was a free 3-part video series teaching at home back exercises to reduce back pain fast. He made it obvious that he was the only local chiropractor to offer the benefits his target audience wanted.

What were the results? Instead of one prospect being generated per month, he had 155 prospects in just one month. Instead of gaining a new patient every month or two, he gained 41 patients in this one month.

This success came from simply changing the strategic message in his Facebook ads and not spending any additional monies. We simply followed and applied the Conversion Equation, and this made all the difference.

This is why every small business needs to use the Conversion Equation.

Dr. Joshua trained his prospects on the relevant and important issues they needed to know when choosing a chiropractor, so his prospects knew what to ask for when seeking a chiropractor's services.

Now, you have the basics of the Conversion Equation.

Earlier I said that a big mistake a small business owner makes is that they do not know the fundamentals required to successfully market their business and attract as many new prospects as their business can handle. I have now shared the fundamentals of the Conversion Equation with you, so you too can out-market and out-sell your competition.

Once again, look at your marketing. Does your current marketing sound the same as the kind of marketing this chiropractor was using? Is your marketing filled with worthless and meaningless platitudes? Like my client family member, Dr. Joshua, are you not generating all the leads your business can handle because of marketing wrong?

This will all change when you apply the Conversion Equation in all marketing platforms from your business card to your emails, website, ads, etc. you will have fast financial results.

Since you picked up this book, I am guessing you want more qualified prospects. If so, you must follow the Conversion Equation: interrupt, engage, educate, and offer.

Before we move on, let me share one more case study to inspire you.

CASE STUDY—THERAPIST AND MINDSET COACH

This client family member is a therapist and mindset coach. Dr. Diana specializes in helping women whose husbands are divorcing them, to let go of anger, and to move on. The women who come to her are hurt, angry, and they have low self-confidence.

Her website looked like most therapists and life coaches. It had her photo and a logo at the top of her home page. No headline interrupted prospects. It said, "Advice for Women from Dr. Diana." Seriously, do you think that has an emotional hot button for a woman who is suddenly finding out that her husband wants a divorce? Do these women care that Dr. Diana gives advice? Aren't they desperately seeking a solution to their problem?

You have to start by interrupting your prospects by talking about the problem they are experiencing. Then you must have a subheading that instantly engages the prospect. You have to show them you have a solution to their problem.

- Interrupt is the headline.
- Engage is the sub-headline.

This formula must be applied to every form of marketing, including your website. The generic "Advice from Dr. Diana" addresses no problem. Why would her target audience pay attention at all? Her website did nothing to engage her prospects, so they leave her website as they are not interested in her advice.

The latest research shows that the typical prospect who visits a website remains on the site for just three to five seconds. If you do not interrupt and engage your prospect in this short amount of time, they are gone.

As a reminder, the third component of the Conversion Equation is to *educate*. You must educate a prospect as to why you are so different than any competitor.

We changed Dr. Diana's website with an interrupting headline and an engaging sub-headline. Then she educates with a short video and makes a compelling no-risk offer. Her target audience is compelled to enter their name and email to find out more. Her offer gets her prospects to download a report titled: *The Secret for Women Who Are Being Abandoned by Their Husbands: Learn the Three Keys to Moving on and Creating Inner Peace.*

The offer is so compelling that it is irresistible to her prospects.

Before re-doing her website, she had no sub-headline either. She simply said, "Download a free report." Can you see why Dr. Diana's website failed to get her qualified prospects and to create income for her practice?

Like almost all business owners, Dr. Diana did not follow the proven *Conversion Equation* in her on-line and off-line marketing—and her marketing was failing—despite the fact she had invested in marketing courses and marketing mentors. No one was teaching or helping her implement the Conversion Equation.

The new headline on her website does interrupt the Dr.'s ideal prospects and they do get engaged because they want more peace. Can you see how the headline and sub-headline work together to interrupt and engage every single qualified prospect who visits her website?

After her prospects are engaged, they watch her video, which is less than two minutes long. They get to see her, hear her, and realize they can trust that she has the solution they desperately desire. They are compelled to take her up on her offer and download her report. She captures their email and their name to continue to market to them with valuable educational information even if they do not instantly become a patient.

This one change with Dr. Diana's website gave her immediate leads, sales, and cash flow.

The Conversion Equation will work for your business, too. If you want to get leads and be positioned as the dominant force in your market, use the Conversion Equation.

Now, let's generate leads fast!

CHAPTER 2
REVOLUTIONARY NEW LEAD GENERATION SYSTEM PROVEN TO WORK

Take a moment and reflect on your business over the last 12 months. Can you tell me the exact number of leads and sales you have made? Many business owners I speak with have not tracked that information. That needs to change. I will create a sample business to show you just how important it is to track your leads and sales.

Let's say that this business had 1000 leads in the past year, and the average conversion rate was 25%. Let's also say the company sold a $100 item, and customers bought 10 of these throughout the year and that the profit margin per sale is 25%.

Doing the math, this company would be earning $62,500 annually. What if this business increase five key business areas? More leads, more conversions, more transactions, higher prices, and more profits. Things might just get more interesting.

If we increase each area by a mere 10%, the annual revenue would almost double from $62,500 to over six figures!

When I work with a client family member, instead of a mere 10% increase in each area, we can typically increase each area up to 50%. So, let's do that math in our previous example. This same business would now go from $62,500 to almost half a million dollars annually! If you think 50% gains in each area would be next to impossible, let me assure you that a 50% increase is child's play. Let me prove this to you.

By asking new client family members about the source of their leads, they typically tell me "word of mouth" or "referrals." Neither of these is reliable, consistent, nor dependable sources as you cannot generate them whenever you want. That is no way to run a profitable business.

Is Your Website Generating Leads?

If you are in business, I am guessing you have a website. Do you know exactly how many leads your website generates every month? Do you know with 100% certainty how many sales your website produces every month? Have you ever wondered why your website is not generating leads or closing sales for you? Here are the hidden secrets that marketing consultants do not want you to know.

The real key to successful marketing is that you must enter the conversation taking place in your prospects' minds, in their hearts, in their feelings and emotions. You must stand empathetically in their shoes. You must know the number one question that is on your prospect's mind. How do you do this?

Every prospect has a problem they do not want, and they desire a result they do not currently have. When you know the actual problem your target audience has, and you can provide the result they want, you simply *use* the Conversion Equation in all your marketing.

The secret lies in my proprietary Core Unique Positioning Statement®, which I will help you create for your business later. For now, just understand that everything you say and everything you do must address the problem your prospects have that they don't want. When created and implemented correctly, this statement allows you to do this verbally, in writing, and in videos, on-line and off-line, too. Once your own Core Unique Positioning Statement® is created, you will stand alone in your marketplace. This statement will clearly and quickly show the right qualified prospects that you and your business are the only logical choice. When you are so different from your competition, with your well-crafted statement, you will generate leads with ease.

Innovation

Your business must innovate and be unique. The entire purpose of your Core Unique Positioning Statement® (CUPS) is to help you to stand out from the crowd. And when you make an offer, that offer must be so compelling and so irresistible that your prospects cannot turn it down.

Here's the problem. Because of the saturation of marketing messages today, most prospects have become numb to most marketing messages they see or hear. The Conversion Equation can drastically overcome this problem. Yet, you will still need multiple touchpoints before your prospects buy what you sell.

How many touchpoints? It takes anywhere from 20 to over 100 touchpoints before a prospect makes their buying decision. Don't worry! When you follow the Conversion Equation, you will reduce the number of touchpoints to about 5-10 points of contact. You can easily make that many contacts when you follow-up with prospects to position your business as the dominant force in your industry as part of your lead generation system.

You may be wondering how do I get my message in front of my prospects 5-10 times? You do this with your compelling offer so that you a prospect gives you their contact information, which includes at a minimum their name and email address. Then you drip valuable educational contact to them regularly by email.

Think about this. While you want people to buy now, about 99% of prospects are not in the market today to buy what you sell. So, when a business offers a free consultation, a discount, a coupon, a free assessment, a complimentary quote, or simply says "call us," they are only appealing to the 1% of buyers ready to buy now.

The other 99% of prospects are only searching for information because they want to determine who is offering the best value. Prospects don't shop price—they shop value!

Prospects consider price only because most businesses do not give them any other value proposition to consider except the price.

The Core Unique Positioning Statement®

Let's go one step further into the Core Unique Positioning Statement®. This is how we make your business unique. While your competitors will all look the same, your business will stand out.

I invite you to do a little research: Do most of your colleagues' websites look the same? Do they all have a generic headline, and are they trying to be all things to all people? Almost all websites are missing the fundamentals we discussed. They have no Core Unique Positioning Statement®. Instead of using a squeeze page as one single page that explicitly addresses only the one problem they are solving, they have a website talking about everything they do.

As I said earlier, the revolutionary lead generation system begins by having you enter the conversation taking place in the hearts, on the minds, and in your prospects' emotions. They have a problem they want to get rid of. They want a result they do not have.

Let's say I am your ideal prospect. Your headline and subhead show me that you understand my exact problem. I see that you have a solution that no one else has. You have addressed what I am truly looking for, so I am instantly compelled to give you my name and email.

When you show me that you truly understand my pain or my problem and have the exact result that I want and then you present me a no or a low-risk offer, I will happily give you my name and email. Now, keep in mind 99% of the prospects who give their name and email are not necessarily looking to buy today and most prospects do not buy until they have been exposed to your messaging somewhere between 5–10 times. Remember, I shared this with you before. The secret to effective marketing, and this proven revolutionary lead generation system is to offer what most prospects truly want.

What is that? Low or no-risk education and information.

The Low or Zero-Risk Solution

Prospects want a low or zero-risk solution to their exact problem. They do not want a phone call as they fear the call will be a sales pitch. By asking only for their name and email for something that appeals to the most ideal prospects (more on this later), you are taking away any fears they have. This results in massive lead generation for your business.

Instead of a complex website use a squeeze page, also called a landing page or an opt-in page instead of a website. The page will not have your photo, or your logo, or any navigation buttons. All those things complicate the website and distract a prospect. The squeeze page only has one action that your prospects can take, which is to enter their contact information to access your no or zero-risk informational offer—one that provides them with proof that you can actually get them the results they are looking for.

◎ CASE STUDY—HEALTH AND WELLNESS PRACTITIONER ◎

One of my client family members is a health and wellness practitioner. She was generating some leads from her website when she hired me. Before she began to use my lead generation system, she was averaging 50 leads a month from her website. She had been using pay-per-click ads to drive traffic to her website. Of the 50 leads, only 3 people scheduled health and wellness consults with her, and from those 3 leads, she was able to convert only one new patient a month. This barely covered her ad spend. She was frustrated and did not know what was wrong.

After I helped her create an optimal squeeze page with the right messaging and format, we stopped her Facebook ads and reduced her marketing costs. Instead, I had her simply drive organic free traffic to her squeeze page by implementing the Conversion Equation. I helped her create compelling social media posts, crafted emails to send out, and invite people she met at on-line and off-line networking events to grab a consult with her.

One month later, using the squeeze page, and applying the Conversion Equation to her marketing with my help, she had 200 leads. These leads are qualified prospects who requested her report and wanted her secrets. Her offer was compelling for them.

Most businesses will only convert 1% of leads to new customers, which is a pretty sad statistic. However, the Conversion Equation is a revolutionary lead generation formula that also positions qualified prospects to become buyers. Most of my client family members average about 50% lead conversion. My client family member featured in this example transformed her lead conversion by attracting qualified prospects to opt-in to her squeeze page. We had not even begun working on converting leads.

Her numbers transformed in 30 days, and her squeeze page generated 200 leads, and 110 of them requested her offer. That is over 50% of those who came to the page. Then, after they received her secrets, she gave them a way to schedule their private health and wellness consultation with her. In the past, less than 10% of all the prospects who came to her website would agree to her offer of a phone consult. Well, with the Conversion Equation in place and her squeeze page optimized, she now had 61 prospects ask for phone consults!

Each new patient that she closes and is worth $3297 to her. Of the 61 phone consultants, 29 of those prospects became new patients of hers. That is $95,613 in new business in just 30 days using this lead generation strategy—without any ad spend! All I did is make changes to her message and her squeeze page and offer and used the Conversion Equation formula.

Are you getting excited yet about the possibilities for your business? Ok, then…

Back to You!

Let's get similar results for your business! How many leads have you generated in the last 12 months? If you don't know, guess. Of those leads, how many have requested your offer?

We are going to get you more leads. This proven lead generation formula conservatively will generate a 10% opt-in rate. That will double the number of leads most businesses get. If we generated more leads without even improving your conversion rate, your bottom line would increase.

Are you convinced that this is the lead generation strategy you must use?

CHAPTER 3
GET ALL THE LEADS YOUR BUSINESS CAN HANDLE

L et me introduce you to the fastest way to get all the leads your business can handle by expanding the lead generation strategy I presented to you in the last chapter. Before I give you the system, I want to first talk about your foundational sales numbers.

Foundational Sales Numbers

I know you want a conveyor belt of qualified prospects. This chapter will help to do just that. However, to begin marketing and lead generation for many more prospects and sales you must know what I refer to as "foundational sales numbers." These numbers are critical as we grow your business together. Why? When you begin to track these lead generation strategies, you can see how they pay off in three ways. What are these numbers?

- The number of prospects generated by your advertising and marketing
- The conversion rate of qualified prospects to customers
- The average value of each customer over a given period of time

Traditional marketing is based on hunting for a prospect, selling the prospect to purchase your products or services, and then upselling your customers for greater profits. When you create strategic alliances with your customers and joint ventures with businesses that complement yours, you will tap into other people's customer bases. These people will be more likely to become your customers simply because of their association with someone or a business that they already trust.

So, now that you know your foundational numbers let's add another lead generation strategy of joint venture partnership.

Joint Venture Partnerships

A joint venture occurs when two or more businesses come together to share markets or to endorse each other to their customer bases. Usually, this is done on a revenue share agreement, although it does not have to be done that way. Successful joint ventures allow you to get a lot of leads quickly. The key to making this strategy work is to find joint venture partners who have products and services that match your same target market.

As an example, I am a business strategist. I help small business owners grow their businesses. Attorneys also help small businesses establish their enterprises. Accountants also help small business owners with their finances. Business owners who purchase accounting services or legal services may need my help. My business consulting clients may need accounting help or legal help. All of these people would be great joint venture partners for my business.

To begin your list of potential joint venture partners, consider what products or services your prospective clients, customers, or patients buy before purchasing from you. Then make another list of the products or services they are buying during their investment in your offerings. The next step is to identify the products and services they purchase after working with you. You will begin to see your ideal joint venture partner.

Looking at the sequence of establishing a business, first my prospects often have gone to a corporate attorney to set up their entity. Then many of them hire a corporate accountant as income is flowing in and their business is growing. It would make sense for me to have a relationship with a corporate attorney and a corporate accountant.

After a typical client family member has an established business, they may also want a web designer, a copywriter, a virtual assistant, a social media expert, a podcasting service, a printing, and distribution service, a publisher. I can go on and on with all the types of businesses my client family members may want and may need as small business owners—and with whom I can enter into a Joint Venture Partnership.

The Chain Event

Think about your business. Ask yourself what people buy before they buy your services or products, and then during and after they buy your services or products. The answer creates a chain event. Your customers are buying something before they buy from you, and those businesses have the potential to not only endorse your business but also to send referrals to your business. And your customers may buy additional products and services while they are using your products and services and after they have purchased from you. Knowing what they buy before, during, and after, allows you to establish specific offers to refer people to those businesses who can then reciprocally refer to you. This is a joint venture.

Let me share an example.

⑤ CASE STUDY-REALTOR ⑤

One of my client family members worked with me to develop a joint venture relationship with one business above her in the chain and one business after her. She had only been working with me a short time, and we decided to focus only on two joint venture partners to begin with.

My client family member is a realtor. She worked with me to create her before, during and after joint venture referral chain. Her job was to follow my exact system to the letter to find these joint venture partners.

With just one referral on average every month from a joint venture partner, she has seen a huge change to her business and income. One joint venture partner was a painter who typically found he was painting people's houses who wanted to get them ready to put them up on the market. She also was able to get one referral on average every single month from a mortgage company that she began to refer business to and who in exchange referred business to her. By establishing these joint venture relationships, she was able to increase the number of leads she received plus increase her earnings.

Her average commission on the sale of a home is $30,000. So, if she has only two additional prospects and sells one of those homes now, she is bringing in an extra $30,000. Over the course of a year, that could be $300,000 or more. There is huge potential and profits in this lead generation strategy.

Now let's look at the chain below her. She began to send business to a mortgage broker. She negotiated a 10% referral fee with her. So, if the mortgage broker referred business to my client, she received a 10% commission. On average, she was making an additional $500 per each person she referred to this mortgage broker. Every month she was working to bring the mortgage broker at least one referral, and many months she brought the broker as many as five referrals. Being extra conservative only one referral a month at $500 each would bring her an extra $5,000 per year for simply referring to a mortgage broker she trusted to take great care of her home buyers.

With this joint venture strategy in place, not only is she getting more qualified prospects, she is also creating more revenue and adding more value to her customers. And the numbers we are using are ridiculously conservative.

This strategy is going to work in your business, too.

Putting This Strategy in Action

To make this process work in your business, you first need to identify potential joint venture partners who provide a similar service to you but not the same service. You want to think about all the products and services that your ideal qualified prospects, clients, customers, or patients need before or after they buy from you, as well as during their buying experience with you.

In my experience, even when people want to create joint venture relationships, they have not figured out a way to approach each of these potential partners and do not know how to correctly structure a deal so that they get more qualified prospects and also can earn more money by having these joint venture relationships.

You must identify the people who will make excellent joint venture partners for you and your business—and that you know the correct strategy to use when you approach each potential partner. If you do not do this correctly you will literally spend a lot of time burning through potential joint venture partners unsuccessfully.

Take a moment and think about all the potential joint ventures that could be good a good fit for the service or product you provide.

I always help my client family members identify at least a dozen of these. In some instances, my client family members have been able to identify as many as 20 potential joint venture partners regardless of their industry. So, let's just say that you've identified at least a dozen. Being conservative, how many referrals would you estimate your joint venture partners would be able to refer to your business to make purchases?

If I use the most conservative numbers, my client family members average three referrals every month from their joint venture partners. These are referrals that actually make a purchase of their products or services. That is less than one per week. How much additional revenue do you think that would add to your business monthly? Take that number and multiply it times 12 and see how your annual revenue increases!

Do you remember we talked about creating a highly compelling informational offer that would promise so much value to prospects that they absolutely would do anything to get it?

Let's see how this helps you get more qualified leads, too!

⑤ CASE STUDIES-REALTOR AND ACCOUNTANT ⑤

Back to my client family member, in the realtor case study above. She also offered educational information in her marketing titled *Five Things Every Homeowner MUST Know Before They Put Their Home on The Market.* That offer placed many prospects in front of her and resulted in a huge increase in sales. She sent many new sales to the joint venture relationship that she established with the mortgage broker. She received referral fees each month from this joint venture partner. We then added another joint venture partner, someone who organized closets. When people were putting their house on the market, she told them that they had to really clean out their closets and she referred them to the closet organizer. My client is paid each month from the mortgage broker joint venture partner as well as the closet organizer. This joint venture strategy is resulting in additional income every single month.

I love this strategy and find it to be one of the simplest strategies to generate more leads and more income fast. Why? This strategy can be implemented immediately by any small business owner, and it helps my client family members create instant cash flow right out of the gate.

One of my newest client family members, Rob, is an accountant. In less than 62 days, we could find $79,000 in additional revenue just by using this joint venture strategy. Keep in mind that this is business that will generate year after year after year.

So, now that you know how to generate more qualified prospects with joint venture partners, let's see how to create a strategic alliance with your own customer base and expand your lead generation even faster.

Endorsement Letters

To implement this strategy effectively, I first have all my client family members make a list of their customers who might be willing to write a letter of endorsement. I instruct my client family members to ask these customers to send this endorsement letter to those prospects that their customer has identified as potentially in need of their products or services.

This is a lead generation method that I refer to as "strategic joint venture alliance relationships." This is different from the joint venture partners' method because you will be establishing relationships with your very own customers. These letters can be sent out by snail mail or email to the names that your own customer base provides you of their friends, family, business associates, and colleagues.

Whether sent by snail mail or email, the response to this type of letter is usually much higher than normal because the introduction is made by someone the prospect already knows and trusts. Your conversion rates will also be much higher with this type of approach because the aspect of trust has already been established. Also, suppose you treat your customers who become your strategic alliances well. In that case, they will have a greater likelihood of maintaining a long-term relationship with you, therefore increasing their value to your company.

Let's see how a client family member set up joint venture partnerships and strategic alliances to grow his patient base quickly. Keep in mind, everything I share with you works in all businesses, including yours, if executed and implemented correctly.

⑧ CASE STUDY-DENTIST ⑨

This client family member applied both strategies of joint venture partners as well as customer strategic alliances. He first set up joint venture relationship with a business that is targeting the same prospects that his business is targeting. My client family member is a dentist, Dr. Englass, and he created a joint venture marketing relationship with an orthodontist.

Why did he select an orthodontist? His patients already trust him. If he recommends that they have orthodontic care, they are very likely to listen to him and schedule a visit and a procedure with the orthodontist he recommends. The orthodontist does not do routine dental work. When he told his patients, in a reciprocal agreement, to see Dr. Englass for their dental care, they happily followed his trusted recommendation. Referrals began to occur, and more patients joined my client family member's practice.

If you think about this, it makes sense. One of the most successful joint venture marketing alliances was the alliance between Oral B toothbrushes and almost all dentists in America! Before the strategic alliance with Oral B, dentists gave out gum. The relationship Oral B formed with dentists was a strategic alliance. This alliance gave the dentists something useful and valuable to give away to their patients. As a result, Oral B received the highest recommendation rating from dentists for any toothbrush. This became part of their Core Unique Positioning Statement® and their sales skyrocketed.

Next, I had my client family member ask patients if they were willing to write letters and or to send emails to other people they knew endorsing him.

Twenty-two patients happily said yes. He gained seven patients very quickly from these letters and he included a special tooth whitening service for each of the patients referred to him by his current patients.

Long-Term Success

Developing joint venture partner relationships and customer strategic alliances will build your business and set your business up for long-term success.

The computer industry is a great example of an industry implementing joint venture partner relationships and strategic alliances really well. Software and hardware companies have created alliances and joint venture partners. Subsequently, they have turned into industry leaders simply because they tied their products to another company's complementary product. And they created brand advocates of customers endorsing them as well.

Actually, analyze any successful large company. You will see that a good percent of its history and growth is paved with carefully structured joint venture partners and customers who in some way have become their strategic alliances, too. Always be looking for joint venture partners and setting up customer relationships for strategic alliances. This should become a logical growth strategy as making sure you have a website. It is essential for lead generation.

Trust

Joint venture partnerships and strategic marketing alliances are built on the foundation of trust. Trust is why people choose to do business with one company over another. When you trust a company, you are more likely to give them your hard-earned money. Advertisers recognize this. When they are promoting a new business or want to grow a business, they spend most of their energy building trust.

In our society, we are tired of advertising. We are inundated with ads and overwhelmed with ads. If you think about the companies using paid endorsements from celebrities. They are enlisting a trusted person to endorse their product or service. Why? We believe that if the product or service is good enough for a trusted celebrity, then it is good enough for us, too.

Remember, when you advertise people are not likely to believe what your ad says. They think ads are lies. They don't trust ads.

Endorsements, on the other hand, are believable. Why? If someone else says it about you or your company, and they trust that person, then they are more likely to believe what is said. However, you do not need to go searching for celebrities to endorse your products or services. Here is how to get the same result in your business without paying a celebrity. That is equally as effective in lead generation.

Establishing Your Business as Trustworthy

Joint venture relationships and strategic marketing alliances help your prospects overcome the trust issue because they understand that few people or businesses would put their reputation on the line to endorse a company that wasn't trustworthy.

When another business or person endorses you, prospects tend to trust what they are saying about you and your company, and you have established credibility automatically. No business can exist in a vacuum. Having your business side by side with other well-established and trusted businesses—as well as having your customers as your raving fans—will give your prospective buyers confidence in your business.

Most people think a business wants to take their money and sell them. They tend to resist buying because of this. When you can establish yourself among other trusted businesses—and your customers are happily sharing your products and services with those they know, your business will no longer be viewed as out to get people's money.

The cost of acquiring a prospect and converting them into a customer is the biggest marketing expense your business will have. And the primary goal of all marketing is to generate more prospects, translating into more customers. Most businesses are spending their marketing dollars trying desperately to reach qualified prospects. They are marketing to masses of people hoping the select few qualified prospects will notice them and buy from them. These businesses are wasting their marketing and advertising dollars to reach customers who ultimately are not going to buy from them.

Let's look at how this strategy fails and why you want to replace this with joint venture partner relationships and strategic marketing partners.

Marketing Failures

Imagine your business sends out a direct mail piece to 1000 people. In this example, we will say that your marketing piece costs $1,000 to develop, create, and to mail out. If you get a 10% response (which would be crazy high), you would have 100 prospects due to the mailing. That means you spent $900 on advertising to people who either were not ready to buy from you, did not know you, or maybe they did not even open the letter or had no interest at all in your products or services. They also had no reason to even trust the claims you made in your marketing piece.

Wouldn't it be nice if you could get a 20% response or 30% or even 50% from the same mailer? Your advertising and marketing dollars would go a lot further. This is why you have to create joint venture partner relationships and strategic marketing alliances. Using both of these strategies will generate a lot of qualified leads fast. You will save money and get better results following this advice.

Joint venture partners and strategic marketing alliances eliminate a lot of expense in your prospecting efforts and allow you to focus your time and money on people who are ready to buy. Instead of paying money to get your message in front of everyone, you will be communicating with people who are connected to your established customers or with other established businesses that have already established goodwill and trust with them

Your Step-by-Step Plan for Rolling Out These Strategies

The first step in setting up joint venture partnerships is first determining who and where your prospective customers are. Does everyone need your products or services? Is everyone a prospective customer? Does only a small percentage of the population want and use your product or services?

If you are a grocery store, dry cleaner, a bank, a gas station, or a business similar to them, everyone needs what you sell. We all need fuel, clean clothes, etc. Anyone would have the potential to joint venture with a business like this and make recommendations for that business to their family and friends.

However, if you are a doctor of Audiology, then you need to have joint venture partners who know people who have hearing loss. A speech-language pathologist, a pediatrician, or a gerontologist would be good strategic endorsement partners for your business.

If you are a massage therapist and your client base is mostly female ages 30 to 50, you might form alliances with a gym, a nail salon, or another place where your target market does business. By engaging in two-way cross-promotions with these businesses and serving as joint venture partners for one another, your customer base will grow.

Let's define who is best for you to seek as joint venture partners.

Would you define your customers as general, meaning everyone has the potential to buy from you, like the gas station or grocery store? Or, is your customer base more specific, meaning only certain people will buy from you, like the massage therapist?

If you are a business with a specific customer base, you will first think of all potential joint venture partners in the buying chain above you and connect with them. You will then think of what else your customers buy while investing in your products and services, and you will contact those potential joint venture partners next. Keep in mind, again; you will not be establishing joint venture relationships with competing businesses. They will be businesses a customer buys from while using your products or services.

For example, many of my client family members who engage in my business consulting services also want a life or mindset coach. I established a joint venture relationship with a trusted mindset life-coaching firm for this reason.

After you work on this one strategy, shift your focus to your current and past customers who may own compatible businesses or know other people who want your products or services.

Strategic marketing alliances from your customer base, in my experience, produce excellent collaborations because these people are familiar with you and your business and know that your business will deliver the results you promise.

This will be much easier than the creation of joint venture partners. If you have created them to be your raving fans and loyal advocates, they will want to help your business grow.

Establishing joint venture partner relationships, however, will take a bit more time. Some of these joint venture partners may not know of you and your business. They may not see the advantages of a partnership with your business, and they and may not even have trust in your products or services. It will take a bit of persuasion to set up these joint ventures; yet, these relationships are worth it, as my client family members have seen.

Work on the more complicated task of establishing joint venture partners first and then the easier part of asking your customer base to become your strategic alliances.

Approaching Joint Venture Partners

After you have identified your potential joint venture, I recommend setting up in-person or virtual meetings with them. Because you are going to need to "convince" them and gain their trust in your products and services, you will bring or send them a letter of endorsement from another business with which you have established a partnership. Or if they are the first joint venture partner you are approaching show some of your customer testimonials. If you have any type of cross-promotions that you have created with other businesses, share this information or testimonials from that referral partner. All of these items will quickly establish your credibility and build trust faster.

The advantage of joint venture partner marketing relationships outside of your customer base is that you will be able to expand your business and create more visibility for your business. So, from this point on, always be on the lookout for creative ways of establishing new joint venture partner relationships.

The nature of your business will determine who are the compatible joint venture partners for your business. If you have more specific customers that you serve, establish alliances with businesses with a similar customer base. These types of joint venture partnerships are logical because they help both companies serve their specific customers.

Some examples from my client family members are:

- Massage therapist-Spa
- Personal trainer-Physical therapist
- Insurance Agent-Bank
- Home Builder-Real Estate Agent
- Naturopath-Supplement shop
- Clothing store-Dry cleaner
- Business coach-Copywriter
- Life coach-Yoga practitioner

The list is endless, and opportunity is everywhere.

If your business has a more general customer base like a gas station, you have many opportunities for alliances. Why? Almost any prospective customer would appreciate an offer for a free or discounted meal at a restaurant, or a free or discounted movie, a discount on clothing or groceries or gash or a car wash. If your business provides products or services that most everyone needs or wants, you are in a position to align with many joint venture partners.

Customer Base Alliances

Once you have at least two potential joint venture partner meetings set up, it is time to work on establishing strategic alliances with your customer base.

Step one of this strategy is to create a list of your current and past customers who have customer bases compatible with yours or who might know friends and family who might use your products or services. I suggest you meet with them in person or by Zoom to establish a marketing alliance. Do not expect them all to say "yes." You do not need them all to agree. You only want those who are happy to participate.

When someone agrees to be a strategic alliance, you will ask them to write a letter of endorsement. Then, you will offer to write a letter which they can then modify or approve. Once your client agrees, spend a little bit of time asking them a few questions so you can customize and personalize the letter on their behalf and in their voice.

Ask probing questions about why they do business with your company and why they would endorse your services and products. You want to capture their words and their personal stories and case studies. Next, you will ask them what they would like you to offer as a gift or special or discount to those they refer to you. For example, in my business, we provide our client family member's referrals with a Business Blueprint (www.tlwebinar.com/blueprint) at a large discount and sometimes at no charge. You can offer a free product or service, free trial, discounted product or service, etc. in your business. You want to give their referrals something you do not typically give others.

Remember, you will write the email or the letter for them and send that to them to either approve of what you wrote or modify or tweak it. Once the message meets with their approval, you will ask them to send out the letter by snail mail or by email. If they use snail mail, you will pay to print the letters, envelopes, and for the postage, too.

CASE STUDY—SPA OWNER

Here is an example of a letter of endorsement sent out by one of my client family members that effectively generated leads. I helped her write this letter. This client family member, Sandra, owns a health spa, and one of her endorsement partners, Dr. Donna, is her customer, who is a chiropractor. Sandra wrote this letter after interviewing Dr. Donna and then let her edit the letter. See if you can spot Sandra's Core Unique Positioning Statement ®.

Dear [Chiropractic Patient],

For the last five years, I have been a loyal member of Spa-One. Being in the chiropractic care business, I know how important it is to take great care of your body with regular massage. That's one reason I keep going back to Spa-One. Like me, the owner of Spa-One, Sandra knows health and wellness and is passionate about helping people live pain-free.

She has a knowledgeable staff along with all the latest equipment. Sandra prides herself in keeping up to date on any innovations in wellness and healing.

On top of all that, her entire staff really knows how important it is for us to move our bodies each day and put good clean food and water in our bodies.

I am writing this letter because I want you to know there is a local spa, I fully endorse you to continue your health and wellness journey. In fact, Spa-One guarantees you will be thrilled with your massage, or they will refund your money!

I have made special arrangements with Spa-One just for my clients. When you make an appointment with Spa-One this month, tell them I sent you and you will receive a free chair massage and a bottle of their special coconut oil massage lotion, too!

Sincerely,

Dr. Donna

Use this example to create your letter from it.

Cross-Promotions

When you establish your joint venture and your strategic alliance relationships, I want you to think about how each business and each customer can help each other through cross-promotional efforts. Let's see how this works.

Before I explain the concept to you, let me ask you a question. Have you ever gone to a major sporting event like a football or a baseball game and looked at the back of the ticket? The back of the ticket will almost always have a coupon for a free hamburger at Wendy's or Burger King or money off a pizza at Pizza Hut or something like this from a large national chain. The large companies have a lot of money to spend on advertising and marketing; yet, they still recognize and take advantage of every opportunity to participate in cross-promotions.

Here is how a cross-promotion works. When two or more companies piggyback each other's various promotions on the same ad piece or marketing piece, they cross-promote each other's business.

I recall going to a Broadway show, and on the back of the ticket, I saw an offer from a New York restaurant near the theater. The offer was for a free appetizer if I went to the restaurant after seeing the show. I am guessing the restaurant paid for part of each ticket for adding their promotion to the back of the ticket. This means the theater saved money on the printing cost of the tickets and the restaurant saved money on advertising. I have used these types of promotions and helped my client family members to use them as well. These types of joint venture cross-promotion relationships can have a 50% or greater response rate!

A large number of leads and customers typically happens with cross-promotion and money is saved on advertising simultaneously.

Imagine if I go to the restaurant to get a free appetizer as offered on the back of my theater ticket. Once I am there, I order a cocktail. Maybe I even decide to have an entrée. Perhaps, I saw the show with my friend, and we both go to get our free appetizers. We both order cocktails with our free appetizers. What if we both also decide to order entrées and maybe even a dessert? We spend a lot of money at the restaurant. And if we liked our meal, we may return, and we will certainly tell friends and family about our positive experience. At the same time, the theater is saving printing costs with the restaurant paying for some or all of the ticket printing.

This is the beauty of cross-promotion, and it works in every industry if you are innovative.

Keep your eyes open. Cross-promotions are being used everywhere. I have consulted with many Fortune 500 companies as well as the smallest start-up businesses. Cross-promotion works for all of them and keeps them busy with qualified prospects and inexpensive marketing.

I love cross-promotions because they build your business fast while saving you marketing dollars. Cross-promotion allows you to get your message in front of the right target audience. A good cross-promotion campaign will distribute your message for low or no cost.

Cross-promotion is a great way to have effective marketing that is efficient in reaching your ideal prospects. These relationships also build trust. When another company connects its brand to your brand, trust is created.

When I first started as a business consultant, I did a cross-promotion with Joe Vitale. When people saw that Joe Vitale was endorsing and cross-promoting me there was instant trust. I went from a newsletter list of about 1,000 to 57,000 overnight with one cross-promotion! That is a lot of new prospects. The more you cross-promote, the more your business will be trusted. I promoted Joe Vitale to my list, and at my events as well because I know him and like him and trust him.

Instead of doing mass marketing, cross-promotion gets you in front of a highly targeted audience. Because of this, you can afford to give away much more value than if you did a general mass-market promotion.

I have client family members who use this strategy regularly. In some cases, their audience is so niched, they can afford to give a free offer or a big discount to a specific number of qualified prospects. Prospects love cross-promotions because they are getting free or heavily discounted products or services from a business even if they weren't thinking of buying from the company. Like the restaurant example, I went to a Broadway show, not expecting to get free appetizers at a local restaurant following the show. It just showed up. It felt like free money to me!

The right cross-promotions are effective because they bring trusting, ready to buy, happy prospects to your business. These people are excited and eager to do business with you because they have been offered real value. Most of these prospects may become long term customers because you treated them right.

So, how do you apply the concept of cross-promotion to your customer base and your strategic endorsement partners? It's simple: Look at who your customers are.

One of my client family members, Jason, owns a roofing company. He is seeking more customers who need a new roof, and I live in an area where most of the homes were built over 30 years ago. Most likely, my neighbors need a new roof now or in the very near future. Jason was happy to send out strategic endorsement letters on my behalf as he had more than doubled his income with my marketing consulting help. I prefer always to establish win-win relationships, and I knew Jason did great work because he had so many happy customers endorsing him. I offered to also send out an endorsement letter on his behalf to my neighbors, and several of them used his services.

What about your customers? Can you help them in some way? Even if they do not own a business, is there some way for you to cross-promote an organization they are part of, a company they work for, a non-profit they enjoy? Creativity and innovation make the cross-promotion concept work.

⑤ CASE STUDY—BOUTIQUE OWNER ⑤

There are so many case studies to choose from as my client family members successfully use this strategy. They establish new ways to cross-promote their companies' products and services constantly. I picked this case study to help you see possibilities and your business's potential to apply this strategy.

My client family member owns a boutique called Sprice! Sprice! specializes in leisure clothes for women, ages 20-40, working from home, yet want to look good on video conferencing. Comfort is a priority for these women. They want to have clothing that fits perfectly and is comfortable without paying a lot of money to do so. Their target market does not want to shop at a department store and be helped a young girl who knows nothing about her work at home needs. Sprice! selected a women's shoe store for their first cross-promotion with. This store's target market is the same as Sprice!'s.

Their cross-promotion piece is a coupon given to the shoe store's customers with their receipt as they leave the shoe store. At the top of the coupon is a cross-promotion that explains that this discount is being given to them as a gift from their store to Sprice!. The shoe store looks great to their customers because they are giving something away that their customers didn't expect. Sprice! wins because their target market now knows where to get their comfortable work at home clothes.

Sprice! paid for the printing costs of 400 coupons. The coupons were designed on their computer and then printed at Kinkos. The printing cost was about $40. Sprice! They also had a coupon for the shoe store that they gave out with each customer receipt driving traffic to the shoe store and creating goodwill to her customers.

This cross-promotion was Sprice!'s most profitable advertising ever. Soon Sprice! was seeking other stores to cross-promote. They loved the fact there was almost no cost to this strategy.

They also asked their customer base to send out endorsement postcards pre-printed with bulk pre-paid postage to those they knew saying they loved Sprice! If a customer came into the store with this postcard, they would get a free scarf. Every time someone brought in a postcard Sprice! would ask who gave that card to them. This customer was also rewarded with a free scarf.

Sprice! had many repeat customers, and they knew their customer base fairly well. For example, one of their customers owned a make-up store. Sprice! offered to do an endorsed mailing for them and asked them if they would be willing to do the same thing for them. Win-win strategy! Sprice! formed another strategic alliance with a customer who owns a tea shop, and that endorsement cross-promotion was a buy-one-get-one-free offer where if a Sprice! customer got one box of tea from the tea shop they got another free. Sprice! used a discount strategy for the tea shop's customers. When a tea shop customer redeemed their gift coupon at Sprice, they got 40% off anything in the store.

This strategy works with all types of businesses. Their customers appreciate the business giving away the free item or the discount for giving them a gift. And your customers are more endeared to you when you also are helping them.

I like to use coupons for cross-promotion strategies. They are easy to create from your computer and printing them on colored card stock paper will make them look great and keep your cost low. Just add your partner's logo and the words, "Compliments of" on the coupon, and do the same for those businesses or customers who engage in your business strategy. This makes the promotion an exclusive for customers of each business or your customers.

No matter what type of business or industry you are, in this strategy works. My client family members in brick and mortar businesses use this at their cash registers or check-out counters while other businesses I consult with use this strategy on-line. Online businesses use a promotion code on their websites instead of a physical coupon.

Take these concepts seriously because they can bring a lot of qualified prospects to your business fast with no or low expense. Adopt what you have learned in this chapter and implement them right away if you want more qualified prospects fast. You will be thrilled with the results.

CHAPTER 4
THE INSTANT CASH FLOW FIX

In the previous chapter, I introduced you to the term "core foundational sales numbers." I reminded you that your business must track these three foundational sales numbers to be successful and consistently profitable. Here they are again:

- The number of prospects your marketing and advertising generates
- The conversion rate of prospects to customers
- The average sales value of each customer

To grow your business and increase your profits, you must keep close track of these numbers on a regular and consistent basis.

I am always amazed when speaking with small business owners who are not aware of these numbers and do not regularly track them. In my experience, this is why so many business owners spend a lot of time and waste a lot of money on marketing that is not effective.

In this chapter, we will solve your cash flow problems with a greater understanding of tracking.

The Big Shift

It is time for you to learn how to stop competing on price forever and to sell your products or services for what they are worth. You will save money on marketing and advertising. Plus, you will cut costs and have more cash on hand.

By using the proven strategies and tactics in the *Conversion Equation*, you will have more qualified prospects. You will also convert a higher percentage of those qualified prospects into paid customers. My client family members see their advertising response increase to more than 100 times. The Conversion Equation will also show you how to increase the amount of your average sale. You will keep customers longer and get more referrals from happy customers.

Being in control of your marketing means you will cut costs and get better results from your marketing dollars. The Conversion Equation is very different from traditional marketing in that traditional marketing only focuses on increasing your number of prospects. The Conversion Equation shifts away from this and is a successful strategy because it is based on these three foundational sales numbers.

Think of it as a formula for your business success. When you implement this proven formula, your business's bottom line will increase from 3-5 times or more when even minor improvement is made to the three foundational sales numbers.

Your business's financial success is determined by your ability to consistently attract a lot of qualified prospects to your company and then to have those prospects become your customers. These prospects can come to a website, a webinar, find your business on social media, come to your store, call your shop, etc. You might do a combination of advertising and marketing to generate prospects. Once you have generated a qualified prospect, you will have a process to "close" them and convert them into paid customers. Closing is simply matching a prospect with a product or service your business offers. It is not hard selling, pitching, overcoming objections, or manipulating them.

So, why is tracking your foundational sales numbers important? When you track the actual dollar-amount spent by each customer, your business can determine if you are filling all of your customer's needs—or provide additional products and services and increase your bottom line.

To grow your business like never before and to cut your costs of doing business, you need to get serious about tracking your foundational sales numbers. For right now, it is ok to guess your approximate closing rate and average sale if you do not know these numbers.

Once you start tracking the number of qualified prospects and the number of sales closed, you will determine your "closing rate." This number is arrived at by dividing the number of customers into the number of prospects. To determine the average revenue generated per customer, divide the number of transactions into the total revenue generated.

As I said, it is acceptable to guess if you have not been tracking these numbers. However, you will want to begin a tracking system immediately. This is a great way to cut costs and create more success in your business.

How to Track

Let's say your business is doing some form of marketing and advertising to get more qualified prospects. Each week you measure the number of prospects your business has received.

For tracking purposes, let me define what a "prospect" is and what a "customer" is so that we are on the same page.

A *prospect* is anyone who comes to your store or shop, calls your business, fills out a web form, comes to your website, messages your company on social media, listens to a presentation, watches a webinar, etc., or asks for additional information about your business. Basically, this is anyone who responds and shows interest to your invitation to do business with your company. A *customer* is defined as someone who purchases a product or service from your business.

Your business will track prospects and customers from now on. You will also be tracking the average revenue generated by a new customer. You arrive at this number by calculating the actual transaction amount of a customer's purchase, adding in any additional items that are upsold to your customer. You will also want to determine how many times a typical customer makes a purchase over the course of a year so that you will know how much a typical customer invests in your products and services yearly.

The Conversion Equation helps you increase all these numbers as you cut costs on ineffective marketing and advertising. These foundational sales numbers are the building blocks of your business. The more you are precise with these numbers, the better.

As I already said, this approach is very different from traditional marketing because your foundational sales numbers will work to grow your business in three ways. Traditional marketing usually has only one strategy, which is to increase the number of prospects. It does not focus on transactions or average sale per customer.

Example

Using simple numbers, let's illustrate how this works. If your business currently has 100 prospects and 50 of them purchase your products or services, you will have a closing rate of 50%. If the average transaction is $100 per customer, your total revenue generated will be $5,000.00.

With traditional marketing, we get the following results. Let's say we get an increase of 10% in the area of attracting prospects. This means this business will go from 100 prospects to 110 prospects. If we do not improve the closing rate and that stays at 50%, we will have 55 new customers.

Let's also keep the average transaction amount the same, at $100. With 10% growth of new prospects, the total increase to this business is $500. The total revenue generated will go from $5,000 to $5,500. That is a 10% increase in revenue and not that exciting to me.

That is what traditional marketing focuses on—only increasing the number of prospects. The Conversion Equation, one the other hand, increases the foundational sales numbers in all areas instead of just one.

Now, with the same example now applying the Conversion Equation formula of growing this business *3 ways instead of just 1 way*. With a 10% increase in prospects, the business will go from 100 prospects to 110 prospects. Again, we are using very conservative numbers for this example. The closing rate also goes up 10% from 50% to 60%, and this now results in 66 customers instead of 50 customers. Finally, we increase the average transaction amount by 10% from $100 per transaction to $110 per transaction. By growing each of these areas only 10%, the revenue increases from $5,000 to $7,260. That is an increase of 45% more revenue! Can you see why we focus on all three numbers instead of only increasing prospects?

I get excited when I see my client family members' results when they increase all three of these numbers. They also realize they can decrease their marketing and advertising expenses or at a minimum maintain them. Any increase in your conversion rates and your average ticket sale goes right to your bottom-line profits, too. This is how we put more cash in your pocket.

Begin this week. Track the current number of prospects to your business per week, the number of prospects your business closes each week, and determine your current prospect to customer ratio and the current average sale per customer.

Just by tracking your foundational sales numbers, you, like my client family members, will see some improvement. I recommend keeping a scorecard of these numbers visible so you can see your bottom-line growth all the time.

I have seen many of my client family members quickly increase these numbers 10%, 15%, 25% and even 50%. or even higher. Remember a 10% increase in all of your foundational sales numbers will improve your bottom line by more than 45%. A 20% increase, which is entirely doable, in all three areas will double your bottom line.

⑤ CASE STUDY—WEIGHT LOSS DOCTOR ⑤

Dr. Sheri is a medical doctor specializing in weight loss. When she first became my client family member, she was not tracking her foundational sales numbers. She did not know how many calls came in per month or how many inquiries were coming in from her website.

We put the Conversion Equation in place, and she began to generate more leads. We tracked how many qualified prospects came in from her marketing and advertising each week. We made two changes to her sales process. This was to send a Consumer Awareness Guide about losing weight to each inquiry who had not become her weight loss patient. She also had her receptionist make a follow-up call to each prospect offering a free consult by phone to see if she could help them lose weight.

These activities increased her sales by 25%. What is really significant is that she had a huge increase in her profitability, too. Her expenses to implement this strategy did not go up. She used the same website and Facebook ad that she was using, and she already had a receptionist in place. We simply optimized leads being converted into paying patients. There were no additional marketing expenses incurred.

The Conversion Equation is unique because it helps you leverage your existing marketing assets rather than always focusing only on the acquisition of new prospects. Best of all, you keep more money when using this proven formula.

Of course, selling is a critical component of your marketing, and when you are able to close more sales, your business will see a tremendous increase in both revenues and profitability. Just by tracking sales, my client family members have seen significant revenue and profit increases.

⑤ CASE STUDY—MARRIAGE COUNSELOR ⑤

This client family member is a marriage counselor. She got almost all her prospects through a book she wrote and gave away on her website and through her social media accounts. She did not follow-up with the prospects who did not purchase her counseling services immediately after getting her book.

We created a drip campaign, which is a series of emails spread out over time, to follow up with these prospects. We invite them to schedule an appointment to see if they were a good fit for her services. With this one additional step she went from a 10% sales conversion to a 40% sales conversion in less than 41 days. Just this one simple change to her sales process increased her sales from about $100,000 to over $800,000 in less than one year.

This is why I stress that you must track your conversion rate, too. If you are using direct mail, ads, online marketing, or any other form of marketing and advertising you will want to know how well it performs. Then, if necessary, you can tweak it to close more sales and generate more prospects. Otherwise, you will be spending money on marketing and advertising that might have high costs and low profits. You will be cash-poor and risk going out of business.

Always measure your conversion rate and try to improve it.

Increasing the Value of Each Customer

Upselling is used in almost all businesses. Think McDonald's. Their employees were trained to ask, "Would you like fries with that?" That is how they strategically increased the transaction of each purchase.

When you purchase an appliance or a car, you are often asked to purchase a warranty. This is another form of upselling. If you purchase a new outfit the store may also offer you shoes to match the clothing that you are purchasing. Again, that is an upsell to increase the size of the transaction. When you make a purchase from a website, Amazon, for example, they recommend other products to go along with your purchase. Yes, that too, is an upsell to increase their transactions and is being done strategically.

To have more cash in your business and to cut costs you do not need to upsell all prospects to make a lot more money. You can get a big increase to your bottom line with upselling only a few prospects each week upsold.

Think about your best-selling products or services. What can you upsell with those? Let me share a case study to help you think creatively about this idea.

⑤ CASE STUDY—LEADERSHIP TRAINER ⑤

My client family member presents on-line and off-line workshops on leadership. She told me every prospect who became a customer was worth $1,000 to her business. I asked her what else could she offer these buyers at the point of sale. She determined she could sell them a guidebook to help them get more out of her workshops. We put this strategy in place by having her simply offer the guidebook on her website. When a buyer was in the process of purchasing their workshop ticket, the guidebook was offered to them. She found that over 15% of the ticket buyers added in her $49 guidebook. This was a special only available at this price at check out. If they wanted to add the guidebook after the sale the price was $129. The "deal" had to be added as an immediate add on at the point of purchase.

Any business can upsell and should upsell. Just make sure your add-on is of high value to your customers. I recall hiring a closet organizer a few years back.

When I hired her, she told me I could add on a kitchen organization session for an additional $250 at this time. That was an upsell. She had a second logical upsell offering which was a quarterly service to maintain my organization systems. She offered me both at the point of sale and I said "yes" to the quarterly service for an additional $250 per quarter. I also agreed to the kitchen organization. Her sale went from the original $500 I was spending for closet organization to double, $1,000, with the her two upsells. She doubled her sales!

Upselling is one of the most underutilized, yet predictably, effective techniques you can use to instantly improve the average value of every sales transaction and to make more money fast.

CHAPTER 5

CHANGE FROM TACTICAL TO STRATEGIC APPROACH

There are two main components to marketing. One is called "strategic marketing," and the other is called "tactical marketing." Strategic marketing is defined as the content of your message. It is not only what you say, it is how you say it, what ideas you focus on, how you communicate those ideas verbally and in writing, as well as, the tone of your messaging.

Tactical marketing is everything you do to execute your marketing strategy. Tactics include having a website, a podcast, blogging, direct mail, social media posts, Facebook or pay-per-click ads, networking, attending trade shows, joining referral groups etc.

When I ask a prospective client family member what they are doing for marketing, I almost always get a list of tactics. Tactics are not part of marketing that makes marketing effective. The key to successful marketing is to master marketing strategy. While both parts of marketing are important, the real leverage comes from strategic marketing.

Most times, when a tactic fails people blame the marketing medium. They believe their ad did not work, their email was not right, or their webinar missed the mark. In the meantime, they have no strategy in place for the marketing they are doing. Usually, I find the lack of strategy, and not the tactic is their real problem.

The Conversion Equation will show you how to say things in a way that will make a huge difference in your marketing results and is based on strategic marketing first, tactical marketing second.

The Real Purpose of Marketing

There are two questions to ask yourself before we go any further:

- Do you know the real purpose of marketing?
- What do you want marketing to do for your business?

Here are the answers that hopefully come to mind: The result of marketing is to facilitate a prospects' decision-making process. There are people out there who need the products and services your business provides. However, you will need to educate many of them about why they need to buy what you sell. Some of them will know they already want to buy the products and services you offer and decide which business to purchase from. These people might have some concerns or objections or questions that must be handled before investing in your products or services.

You are the expert at what your business provides. Your prospective customer does not know the key points surrounding their purchase. Because of this they really do not know how to make the best decision. When they are not informed, they will choose the lowest price product or service because they see that as the best deal.

Big Opportunity

Let me give you an example to show you where the big opportunity lies for you.

I have decided to remodel my kitchen. I have never done this before, and I have no idea whatsoever who to hire for this job. I cannot tell the difference between a remodeler's quote for $50,000 to the one I got for $100,000. These quotes look the same to me. I am clueless about this purchase and it is a large investment.

How does this relate to your business and marketing? Most people are this clueless about purchasing your products or services as I am about hiring a kitchen remodeling company, no matter what products or services you are selling.

The job of marketing is to facilitate your prospect's decision-making process. All prospects and all customers want to feel confident that their hard-earned money has been well spent. They want to know that they have made a good investment and the right decision to spend their money on your products or services. These prospects not only want the best price, but they also want to get the best deal. This means they want to know they will receive value when making the decision to part with their money.

As a marketer, (and any small business owner must be to some degree, you must find out what is most important to your prospects. You cannot afford to guess at this like most business owners do. Once you know what is truly important for your ideal prospects, you can educate them on the best deal when it comes to buying the kinds of products and services your business offers.

The more quantifiable proof you provide that your business offers them the best value and deal, the faster they will convert from prospects to customers. Your marketing must be communicated to them, so they pay attention to your message and what you are saying. Then they will take action on your offer.

No Marketing Strategy

Most businesses do not have a long-term strategy and have not started marketing with an end result in mind. They are just tossing out many marketing tactics and hoping and praying something will stick and will work to grow their business. An end result is the action you want a prospect to take. This action might be coming to your place of business, watching your webinar, opting in for a special report, setting an appointment, having a consult, calling your business, etc.

Another problem is not only doesn't the average business have an end in mind (a strategy). Their marketing messages are filled with jargon, and are they are cookie-cutter, look-alikes of every other company in their niche. If this is the case, the only thing the business can compete on is one thing—price. Suppose your business has no end strategy and your business also looks like everyone else. In that case, prospects will purchase from the lowest price provider in the marketplace because they don't see any value in investing more to get what looks like the same thing.

Know What Your Prospects Want

Before you jump into marketing tactics, you must use some strategic thinking. Unless you take time to understand your prospects and what they truly want to buy and then create a strategy to help them buy, your tactics will most likely fail to get results.

You cannot educate your prospects or spark their decision-making if you do not truly understand your prospects and their problems.

And if your marketing looks and sounds like your competitors, and you are not marketing with the proven *Conversion Equation*. You will not get predictable results with your marketing and will be trying tactic after tactic. And this, as you well know, can be expensive.

If you are always competing on price, then there is no clear difference to your prospects between buying from your business or that of a competitor. You will have to discount your products and services.

Now, let's do a deep dive into The Conversion Equation and change your marketing results forever, so you no longer compete on price.

Remember, strategy before tactics!

CHAPTER 6
CONVERSION EQUATION

Most people do marketing and advertising with a lot of jargon, and they look like a cookie-cutter of all of their competitors. If a prospect is selecting someone to do business with and everyone looks alike, they might do business with the lowest cost provider. Now, we are going to make sure your business does not fall into this trap.

Ask yourself this question and answer openly and honestly, why would anyone choose you over your competition?

As you respond, see what is different and unique about your business versus your competition and then go deeper. Ask yourself if a person hearing, reading, or seeing your marketing and advertising would say "Well, I would hope so" to your claims. My guess is you will find you need to make changes to your marketing and advertising messages. The "well I would hope so" statement is a great way to test if your marketing message is unique.

Here is another great way to test your marketing and advertising messages. Ask yourself this question about your claims, "Who else can say that?" Stop thinking about "Who else can do what I do?" and think in terms of "Who else can say what I say?" If the answer is almost anybody, and everybody can say what I say, then we have some work to do.

Breaking the Identical Marketing Trap

Most businesses' marketing and advertising look virtually identical to all of their competitors. With almost all businesses claims, prospects can say, "Well, I would hope so!" Besides, most businesses can make the exact same claims. If you do not believe me, pull up the websites of five other businesses in the same industry as your business and look at their home pages. Are they saying some of the exact same things you are claiming? Are their websites similar to yours?

Remember, it is not who can do what you do that is important. It is who can say what you say. If your marketing and advertising are full of jargon, then sadly, that answer is all of your competitors can say what you say.

The final jargon detector is what I call the "scratch-out write-in test." Take a look at all of your marketing pieces on-line and off-line. Scratch out your name or the name of your business and write in your competitor's name. If you can do that, your marketing has failed the test.

When I use these tests with my new client family members, almost all of them fail. They discover they have been using jargon and are not standing-out to their prospects. When I fix this problem for them, they then have a huge competitive advantage in their business. Now, it is time to do this for you, too!

The title of this book is *Conversion Equation*, right? It's time to reveal how you can follow a straightforward and proven process—the Conversion Equation. When you do, you will eliminate jargon forever and finally begin to get the results from your marketing that you should be getting, like my client family members are getting.

Diving Deeper into the 4 Components of Conversion Equation

You will recall that I introduced these components in an earlier chapter, and now, I will take you into each of the elements more deeply.

As a reminder, the first component of the Conversion Equation is *interrupt*.

This process gets qualified prospects to pay attention to your marketing and advertising. This is accomplished by affecting your prospects emotionally.

The second component is to *engage*. Once a prospect is interrupted, it is essential to give your prospect the promise that you can help them make the best decision possible to facilitate their decision-making process. This is also best accomplished by using emotion. This makes up the engage" component.

The third component of the Conversion Equation is to *educate*. After you have interrupted and engaged a prospect, you have to give them information that allows them to fully understand how and why you and your business can solve their emotional problems or pain. You do this by providing detailed, quantifiable, specific, information for them. By doing this, you take them from the emotional pain you created when you interrupted and engaged them to a logical buying decision.

Finally, the fourth and final component of the Conversion Equation is *offer*. You have interrupted a prospect based on the problems that are important to them emotionally, then you have engaged them with the promise of a solution to their emotional pain. You have also given them educational information that makes your solution to that emotional problem real and believable.

Now it is time to provide your prospect with a no or zero-risk way to take the next step in your sales process. You make an offer by using a free or zero-cost marketing tool. My client family members have successfully used special reports, Consumer Awareness Guides, brochures, videos, audios webinars, checklists, templates, quizzes, etc. These items educate prospects even more and allow them to feel they are in complete control of the decision-making process.

Attracting Your Prospects

The Conversion Equation is a proven formula that does the job marketing is supposed to do—*interrupt, engage, educate, and offer.* Before you can effectively apply and implement this formula, to sell anything to a prospect, you must step back and look at exactly who your ideal prospective customer is. You must understand them and how they make their decisions. You need to identify the emotional hot buttons that trigger them to buy your product or service, too.

There are three concepts you must take into account when it comes to understanding your prospects fully. These three concepts will make all the difference in your marketing's effectiveness and in your company's profitability. Let's explore them now.

As a clinical psychologist specializing in organizational behavior, I am fascinated with the way people think especially regarding buying decisions. Every human being's brain works on these three concepts that relate to sales. These concepts are *downtime, uptime*, and the *reticular activating system.*

Downtime is the hypnotic state of running automatic patterns that allows your brain to perform habitual tasks without conscious thought. Our brains are in downtime much of the time. Have you ever driven home from work and not remembered the drive and wondered if you stopped at all the traffic lights? That is downtime. Downtime occurs when you are engaged in a habitual behavior that you do so frequently that you do not consciously think about it. Just today, I could not remember if I had brushed my teeth or not! This is downtime.

How does the concept of downtime apply to marketing? People are bombarded with ads on-line and off-line. So, the ads become routine, and their brain stops consciously noticing them. If I am watching a television show and am interested, I pay close attention. When the ads come on my brain goes to downtime.

The second concept you need to understand about the human brain related to sales is uptime. *Uptime* is when the brain is alert and actively engaged. I drove home the other night in a horrific rainstorm. The roads were flooded, and it was foggy. Instead of driving in downtime, I was gripping the wheel hard, and I turned off the radio to fully concentrate on the road. That is an example of uptime. Our brains go into uptime when watching a scary movie, and we just know something frightening is about to occur. Uptime is when your brain is on high alert, as in these two examples.

How does uptime relate to your marketing? When prospects are in uptime mode they consciously stop and pay attention to your advertising or marketing. They are open and curious about your suggestions and solutions. You have gained their attention and they are paying attention to your marketing message. The goal of all your marketing messaging is to snap your prospects out of downtime and into uptime successfully. We want to bring your prospects into full consciousness and to make them aware of what you are communicating to them. Once you understand how to do this, and you will as you continue reading this book, you will have the ability to reach your financial goals.

Finally, there is one more concept you must learn about how your prospect's brain works concerning sales and marketing. This final concept is called the *reticular activating system*. The reticular activator is the part of your brain that constantly scans the environment seeking familiar things, things that are unusual, and problematic things. The human brain is scanning for these things all the time. When the brain detects any of these three things subconsciously, it sends a message over to the brain's conscious side and says, "Wake up and pay attention." The things the brain begins to pay attention to is called an activator.

Our brain, on a subconscious level, is always seeking activators. It is searching for familiar things, unusual ones, or problematic things. These need a conscious response. Whenever the brain finds one of these, it snaps your conscious brain out of downtime and uptime.

Marketing Depends on Waking Prospects Up

When you know what wakes up your prospects, so they pay attention to your marketing message, you can move them from interrupt to the engage stage. Then your chances of selling a prospect have gone up at least one thousand percent! Most marketers only know how to interrupt prospects. They do not know how to engage prospects because they do not know how to use activators. If they do, they do not know how to use the ideal activator for their specific target market.

As I said, most marketers use marketing messages that interrupt, and that is all they do. They forget to engage the prospect's brain once it is awake and out of downtime. When the brain wakes up it quickly, searches for additional, clarifying information. It seeks facts wondering if what interrupted them is really important to them. It becomes curious and wants to see if it needs to do anything with the information it has been alerted to. If the brain finds supporting facts that the messaging is important, the brain becomes alert, awake and engaged. If it finds no relevant data, it goes right back into downtime.

Think of what engages the brain as your prospects' hot buttons. Let's say I am watching a commercial, and it is about baby diapers and I do not have kids or grandkids my brain says, "Not relevant, go back to sleep." On the other hand, if I am watching a commercial for curly hair products and have curly hair, my brain gets interested because it is a hot button issue for me. Activators are important in this formula because they are something that snaps a prospect from downtime to uptime and is based on something that is familiar, unusual, or problematic. An activator can also be classified as a hot button if it is important and relevant to your prospect.

Successful marketing comes from interrupting and engaging your target market by fully understanding and relating to their problems, frustrations, struggles, and challenges. You must then address those issues in your marketing messages. Think of your prospect's pain or problems as their hot buttons. I am not talking about the unethical agitating of a problem. I am talking about ethically tapping into the problems that your prospects already have because you care about helping them with your products and services. You are not making them afraid of a situation they do not have or might not have. You are simply relating to their problems and pointing out those problems. When marketing does a good job of this, a prospect's reticular activating system will notice the messaging and will wake the prospect up to pay attention.

Do not forget that it is essential for you to use activators that will go beyond the interrupt phase and that will target the relevant hot buttons your prospects have. Otherwise, your prospects may have their brains awakened and then find no relevance in your messages. Then their brains will go right back into downtime, and your message will not move them into action.

To show you how this works, let me share an example. I was walking on the beach the other day with my friend, Sheila. Someone yelled out, "Hey, Sheila." She instantly turned around. She was interrupted and paid attention because she heard her name. We both chuckled to find out they were calling out to another person named Sheila. Since her name is an activator, she got interrupted. When she found the person was calling out to another person by the same name she was no longer engaged. She went from uptime instantly back to downtime.

This happens in marketing and advertising all the time. Most marketing interrupts and does not engage; therefore, it only captures attention and interrupts a prospect. However, when a prospect finds out that the message is not based on anything relevant or essential to them, and the message does not solve the prospect's problem, their brain quickly reverts to downtime.

Now you know why most marketing fails miserably and is a waste of time and money because it only interrupts prospects. You now know that the Conversion Equation IS your marketing answer because if you only interrupt a prospect, that is only one-fourth of the Conversion Equation. Your marketing must include all 4 components—*interrupt, engage, educate,* and *offer* to maximize results from your marketing and advertising.

CHAPTER 7
OVERCOME YOUR 3 BIGGEST MISTAKES

One of the biggest mistakes you can make is that you will always be competing on price, as I stated earlier, if you do not engage in professional marketing services. Why? Because without implementing the right marketing process, the price will be the only relevant variable that you are giving your prospects to consider.

However, my goal is for you and your business to become the obvious, logical choice. How do we accomplish this for your business? We do this by implementing the Conversion Equation correctly which will ensure your marketing will be superior to all of your competitors. Your business will stand out from your competition and prospects will choose your business. And you will avoid the biggest marketing mistakes.

Inside Reality and Outside Perception

The other two marketing mistakes are all about perception. We will address these now by looking at your business's two sides, which most business owners never even realize exist. There is one side that I will call the "inside reality," and the other side I call the "outside perception." Inside reality encompasses everything you do. It is everything that makes your business special. This can include *your* unique skills and talents and the skills and talents of *your team*.

Included as a part of the inside reality is how customers are treated before, during, and after the sale. In addition, inside reality includes your businesses' systems, policies, and procedures. It is what your business stands for and stands against. It includes your passion as the business owner as well. When you combine all of these things, they equal the value your business brings to the marketplace.

What is your businesses' inside reality? Suppose you were to ask your customers why they purchase products and services from your company. In that case, I am certain they could tell you quantifiable, specific, and really obvious information about why they are your customers. I know this is true because I very often have my client family members survey their customers to gather this information. Instead of guessing what customers would say, we ask. Their customers can point to specific benefits they enjoy when doing business with their companies, and your customers, when you survey them, will also be able to do this. So, your business's inside reality is all about who you are as a company, what your company does, and who and what you or your company is that allows you to perform better.

How customers and prospects perceive your business is outside perception. It is developed through the interactions that your prospects and customers have with your business. Additionally, your customers will draw on their past buying experiences with your business to form their outside perception of your business.

Here's the problem: If you provide the very best customer service and if your customers love you, none of that matters to your prospects—if they do not even know your business exists. Or if they do notice your marketing and advertising, and because of your lack of knowledge in marketing, you fail to market your business properly, prospective customers will perceive that you are no different, no better, no worse, than your competitors. To them, you are all exactly the same.

In my experience as a small business marketing strategist, I estimate that over 95% of all businesses are completely inept when it comes to marketing. As a result, the inside reality and outside perception are viewed differently.

Regardless of how good you are at what you do and regardless of your inside reality, prospects will not be able to figure out your genuine inside reality based on your marketing. You appear to be just another business that sells whatever it is that you sell. These add up to the three mistakes that must urgently be solved for your business.

Guess what? These three mistakes can also hurt your ability to close a sale, too.

You cannot rely on yourself or a salesperson or sales team to educate prospects on your differences, inside and outside reality, and to close the sale, without overcoming these three marketing mistakes.

⑤ CASE STUDY—FINANCIAL ADVISOR ⑤

A client family member, Suzanne, is a financial advisor. When she hired me as her small business marketing consultant, she was only getting in front of 5 prospects a month. She was closing 2 out of 5 prospects each month and needed to reach more qualified prospects fast to turn her business around. I put the Conversion Equation in place and not only helped her business stand out from all other financial advisors, we shifted the inside and outside realities prospects held about her services. Within less than one month of overcoming her three big marketing mistakes and applying the Conversion Equation in her business, she was seen by prospects who had no idea her financial planning firm even existed. Within less than 47 days she had 23 qualified prospects and was able to close 16 of them.

Your business must also overcome these same three mistakes. You have to be certain qualified prospects know you and your business exist. Your marketing must consistently deliver eager, qualified prospects to your business, so your business thrives and barely survives.

So Many Choices

There is another problem we must consider. There is more competition today than ever before, and your prospects have a lot of choices. They have to sort and sift through many businesses and offers to make a buying decision. And the internet has made the problem significantly worse. There are websites, blogs, podcasts, pay-per-click ads, social media sites, Facebook ads, and more, in front of your prospects all the time. This is very confusing. Most purchasers today start their buying process by researching on-line and become inundated with marketing messages and advertising.

If your business advertises on-line, you are most likely spending a lot of time, money, and energy getting prospects to your website. Sadly, if you are like most businesses, you have the same clichés and platitudes on your website as your competitors. "Service, quality, dependability," etc. You are not saying anything that differentiates your business or tells your prospects why they would and should choose your business.

You can spend a lot of money on ads and Search Engine Optimization (SEO), also called ranking, to get qualified traffic to visit your website. Even if you do get qualified traffic to your website, this traffic rarely converts to buyers because your website does not convert these prospects. The internet is not the answer to your marketing problems. In fact, the internet is simply another place to put out your currently jargon-filled undifferentiated messages that do nothing to facilitate your prospects' decision-making process. Of course, the internet is an important tool in your marketing tool kit, and you do need to have a lead generating website.

First, you must rid your message of jargon forever. You have developed the right strategic messaging and created Core Unique Positioning Statement*, which tells why and how your business is different. It also reflects your inside and outside perception—or your website will also fail. We will be creating this statement soon!

Jargon

Sadly, most business marketing consists of nothing but jargon, which I mentioned early. This concept is so important I want to touch on it again to drill this point home truly. Jargon is not going to bring the brains of your prospects into uptime. Jargon consists of words or phrases that are common and predictable and do not have a lot of meaning to your prospects. Most businesses use jargon in their adverting and marketing and then wonder why they are not getting the desired results.

Within the first 30 seconds of any marketing message, no matter what the medium, written, spoken, video, audio, you must instantly snap your prospect into uptime to have any chance of them responding to your marketing message. Things like "biggest selection," "highly professional," "lowest-priced," "best quality," "best service," "quickest," "most convenient," "plenty of free parking," "most dependable," "We're the experts," "We specialize," "We work harder," "We get to job done right the first time," and "We have been in business for 40 years" are all examples of marketing based on jargon. You see this type of marketing every day both online and off-line and so do your prospects.

Certainly, your business could truly be and do all of those things. That is part of how you do business and what your business is based on. You want to build your inside reality and your Core Unique Positioning Statement®. Why?

If I see a marketing message that says, "best quality" or "fastest service," I quickly pass it by. So do most prospects. The message is commonplace, and the human brain stays in downtime due to a lack of hearing anything unique or important. Your brain will do this too and so will your prospects' brains. What makes your company different does not come through in a message filled with jargon.

You have to avoid jargon in all of your marketing messages, or your business simply looks and sounds like every other business. If you are using jargon in your current marketing and advertising, your business currently sounds like all the rest in your industry. You are not standing out as unique, and your marketing is boring, and your inside reality and outside perception will not match up.

Take a look at the marketing messages you are currently using in your business. Are you using jargon in your marketing? Let's see! We are going to put your marketing messages through a few tests. We did this earlier and the reason I am suggesting you do it again is now you understand the Conversion Equation and downtime, uptime, and reticular activators.

Look again at your current marketing and what you are saying in your marketing and advertising messaging. After each marketing message you are using, ask yourself if a prospect could say, "I would hope so." Think about this. If you say "highest quality" or "professional" as examples, and I am one of your prospects, I would say "I would hope so" as I would expect that feature from any business. My brain would pick up the jargon and would not go into uptime. What a boring message! If your marketing and advertising talk about commonplace things, they lack power and interest, and I am not surprised you do not have a consistent conveyor belt of qualified prospects.

Examples

One of my client family members, John, hired me for marketing consulting, and when I looked at his marketing, it was filled with lame jargon and platitudes. John is a leadership consultant and his marketing message said, "We train leaders to transform. Leaders will learn the skills to increase the performance of their teams." Well, of course, I hope so! Why else would any company ever invest in a leadership consultant who did not do this and who did not give this exact result? That messaging, like most marketing messaging, is a jargon-fest. John did not tell me anything about his company's inside reality. He lacked a Core Unique Positioning Statement® that set his business apart from all of his competitors. The message was boring and built on meaningless platitudes. I was not at all surprised he felt desperate to bring qualified prospects to his business.

As you learned in the previous chapter, marketing professionals have proven processes and use the Conversion Equation to generate qualified prospects. I have been successfully generating qualified prospects for all types of business owners for almost 40 years. Nearly every business I have ever worked with needs to improve their inside reality, create a Core Unique Positioning Statement®, and increase their outside perception. Most of these businesses have a good inside reality; however, they lack a Core Unique Positioning Statement®, and they do not have the right outside perception. So, while they are skilled at their services or provide high-quality products and great value, they look and sound no different from all the other businesses in their industry. Their prospects see no difference between a competitor, so they choose the least expensive option.

Look at your marketing, advertising both online and off-line. Is it instantly obvious, specific, and quantifiable, what makes your business unique? Is it clear that your business is different from all the rest? Do you educate prospects on what they need to consider before making any purchase in your industry and how your business stands alone?

⑤ CASE STUDY—CLEANING COMPANY OWNER ⑤

My client family member, Trisha, owns a cleaning company. She needed more qualified prospects to expand her business, so she hired me to help her. When she first came on board with me, her marketing and advertising were getting almost no results, and she was spending a lot of money and time trying to get more business. I asked her how her business was different and stood out from all the cleaning businesses in her area. At first, she gave me all the typical jargon I expected. I kept asking questions and digging deep to find something she did differently that no one in the industry talked about. The other local cleaning companies might have made the same claim as Trisha, yet none were. This would be her point of differentiation and used in her Core Unique Positioning Statement®.

To stand apart, I helped Trisha to create a Consumer Awareness Guide titled, *3 Deadly Mistakes You MUST Avoid When Hiring A Cleaning Company*. This was a 7-page report explaining the mistakes people made when hiring local cleaners. The report concluded with her telling the points of differentiation that only her company provided. Her cleaning company stood out as the only company that would refund your cleaning service fee if you found they had not done an outstanding job. The client would not pay if they were not satisfied. The report directed the reader to ask that question to any local cleaning company they were considering hiring. We already knew, by our research, no other local company made that guarantee.

Very quickly, she became known as the ONLY local cleaning business that stood behind their work. Her company stood out. In fact, within less than nine months, she had so many prospects, she purchased another cleaning company's business and expanded her workforce and had 200% more business!

The Fix

The issue with almost everyone's marketing is that their outside perception is not an accurate reflection of their inside reality. Let's fix this in your business right now. In my experience helping over 6,000 business owners worldwide, I find that almost all entrepreneurs and business owners are attempting to generate qualified prospects incorrectly. They do not use marketing and advertising that succinctly portray their company's inside reality to prospects, and they lack a Core Unique Positioning Statement®. If you are currently doing the same thing in your marketing and advertising, this is not your fault, and we are going to fix this right now.

Most of us think marketing is what is done in the television commercials we have grown up watching. These commercials are 30 seconds which does not give advertisers enough time to educate prospects about their differences and uniqueness. This is why these short ads on television are filled with slogans. "Just do it," "plop, plop, fix, fix," "snap, crackle, pop,", etc. They are not using any comparative benefits in these 30-second slogan-type ads. There is just no time to do this with the limit of a 30-second commercial constraining the advertiser. This kind of television ad does not illustrate a company's outside perception to reflect its inside reality accurately. It lacks a well-constructed Core Unique Positioning Statement® to help them stand alone in their marketplace.

You will recall that marketing's job is to grab a prospect's attention and snap them into uptime, right? Then, you must quickly facilitate a prospect's decision-making process. Most television advertising is done by large ad agencies representing big companies with huge advertising budgets. These brands have many competitors who cannot afford the kind of advertising and marketing budget they have. So, they win business by default as they get their brand recognized with a large ad spend and through repetition of their slogans.

The big company's inside reality and outside perception do not have to match up. They are not dealing with a lot of competition. They only need to have their ads focus on getting their prospect's attention. They are only going for product recall, and they use slogans to do just that.

Let me prove to you how effective this is. What company is this? A TV commercial from the 1960s had Madge, the manicurist saying, "You're soaking in it." If you were alive in the 1960s most likely you know the answer. How can your brain recall a slogan from nearly 60 years ago? The answer, repetition of the slogan sticks. Repetition advertising with jingles and slogans is expensive and smaller companies cannot afford to use this methodology.

Advertising agencies represent big companies with big pocketbooks who can get away with repetition. When you hear the same slogan over and over again you tend to recall it. Interestingly, Alka-Seltzer ran the "plop, plop, fizz, fizz" commercial, and while people recalled the jingle, they did not recall what the product was! Would you want to spend your hard-earned money on a cute slogan that didn't get a real result?

Guerrilla Marketing

While advertisers were using this advertising approach, small businesses could not. A smaller business needed and wanted to see a return on their investment. In the 1970s, Jay Conrad Levison, later labeled as *"The Father of Guerilla Marketing,"* had built many brands with slogans and jingles for large companies. Some of his most famous marketing campaigns were for the Marlboro Man, the Pillsbury Doughboy, Allstate's good hands, United's friendly skies, the Sears Diehard battery, Morris the Cat, Tony the Tiger®, and the Jolly Green Giant. These companies were able to dominate their market with slogans and jingles because they had the means to do this.

Eventually, these expensive ads became less effective, and consumers became jaded by slogans and jingles. Jay Conrad Levinson was a college professor, and some of his students, including, Bill Gates and Steve Jobs, were taking a marketing course with Jay. They wanted to know how to market their smaller firms on a low budget. As Jay researched this information for them in the library, he realized no one helped smaller companies get their advertising to work, and no one was teaching how a small business could do this at low or no cost. These businesses simply didn't have the budgets large firms had and Jay understood that.

Jay Conrad Levinson decided to write a book titled. *Guerrilla Marketing* shares the secrets marketing professionals knew, and small business owners were clueless about. I had the privilege of co-authoring two Guerrilla Marketing books with Jay. As a Master Certified Guerrilla Marketing Trainer and Coach who had the privilege and honor of co-authoring these books with Jay, *Guerrilla Marketing for Spas* and *Guerrilla Marketing for Beauty Salons*—and as someone who knows how to apply Guerrilla Marketing strategies and tactics correctly, I can tell you with the assurance that Guerrilla marketing works and its concepts are woven into the Conversion Equation that I am presenting for you.

Guerrilla marketing is based on the concepts of using unconventional tactics to get a prospect's brains into uptime using low or no cost advertising and marketing. Guerrilla marketing relies on creativity and not on a big expense account. The basis of Guerrilla Marketing is to be able to create marketing that is shocking, funny, unique, outrageous, or clever, and that wakes a prospect up, interrupts and engages them. Guerrilla marketing took the world by storm and changed how advertising and marketing worked. Even larger companies today use Guerrilla Marketing and most educational institutions teaching marketing and advertising will also teach Guerrilla Marketing concepts.

I have found by professionally combining Guerrilla Marketing concepts with the Conversion Equation, my client family members have a successful and profitable marketing experience. Again, as mentioned in a prior chapter, get the professional help of a marketing consultant who has a track record. I recommend you pick someone who is a Master Certified Guerrilla Marketing Trainer and Coach and who is an expert in the Conversion Equation as well.

CHAPTER 8

FIND $10,000 TO $100,000 IN HIDDEN ASSETS HIDING IN YOUR BUSINESS NOW

There is a huge opportunity in every business to leverage its hidden marketing assets, something I've come to see time and time again as a licensed Hidden Marketing Assets business and marketing consultant. I guarantee that my small business marketing consults—or myself—will find $10,000 of hidden marketing assets if it is a new business if a small business spends 45 minutes of their time on a Profit Acceleration session. If it is an established business, we guarantee in 45 minutes to find them a minimum of $100,000, or we will cheerfully refund the money.

You can check out the offer here (www.tlwebinar.com/blueprint) and take advantage of it right now, too.

How do we do this? We use many strategies, and I will share some of them with you now. All of the techniques work harmoniously to grow your profits.

Increasing Transactions

The purpose of this strategy is to have your prospects to purchase your products or services more frequently than they currently are doing now. Behind this strategy are upselling and cross-selling concepts. Both of these strategies are profit generators!

First, let's define each concept. Remember, I mentioned upselling in an earlier chapter. To refresh your memory, let me use an example that you most likely will relate to: Remember when you placed an order at McDonald's, the sales associates used to ask, "Would you like to supersize it"? This is an excellent example of an upsell. Your purchase now costs more, and McDonald's makes greater profits.

Cross-selling at McDonald's is when the person taking your order asks, "Would you like an apple pie with that?" Instead of a greater quantity or larger size, they offer an additional product that you can add to your order. Both upselling and cross-selling work best at the point of sale when the customer is making their purchase.

Think about it. It would not be logical for McDonald's to ask you to purchase an upsell or a cross-sell after you paid for your burger. You must ask while the customer is making their purchase for these strategies to generate more revenue for your business.

Here is a fact that almost no business owners realize: 34% of prospects will buy additional products or services at the time of their original purchase. The problem is almost no businesses ask their customers to buy additional products or services.

In my experience, this is one of the most lucrative opportunities and will dramatically increase the revenue and profits of your business. This is just one hidden marketing asset I identify and implement strategies for with my client family members.

⑨ CASE STUDY—WEIGHT LOSS PROGRAM CONSULTANT ⑨

One of my client family members sells a guaranteed weight loss program, which is sent by snail mail. It includes a recipe book, guidebook, water bottle, instructions for the program, and a protein supplement. My client family member had not been upselling or cross-selling and hired me to help her create more revenue and profits.

At the point of sale, I had her offer the recipe book, guidebook, and instructions as an instant download for a buyer for only $49 more at the point of purchase. For only $17 a month, the customer could add on an app for their phones that would track their ability to follow the program and give them access to videos each day to help keep them accountable and on track and ensure their success with her program.

First of all, my client family member is capturing the upsell and the cross-sell while her customers are excited about their weight loss, have their credit cards in hand, and are eager to get started. Are you beginning to see the brilliance of this strategy? The result was that 62% of those purchasing on her website said "yes" to one offer, and 23% said yes to both offers.

By combining her hidden marketing assets, Guerrilla Marking, and the Conversion Equation, she quickly had more qualified prospects to upsell and to cross-sell.

⑤ CASE STUDY-DERMATOLOGIST ⑤

Here is another case study using the upsell and cross-sell strategy. This client family member, Dr. Brooks, is a dermatologist. She specializes in skin care services for women ages 35-65 who want to have a more youthful look. Most of her income comes from doing Botox® for these women; yet, she has an opportunity to make a higher profit margin from other services that can be up-sold and cross-sold. I transformed her income by finding out what other services she could provide for her patients with integrity, transparency, and authenticity. I make certain that my client family members do not ever upsell or cross-sell products or services that will not add value to their customers' results.

I had her list all potential products and services she could ethically upsell or cross-sell. Her list included CoolSculpting®, eyelash enhancements, laser hair removal, laser treatments, microdermabrasion, chemical peels, photodynamic therapy, skin cancer treatment, Moh's micrographic surgery, tattoo removal, and vein therapy. She told me that most of her current revenue came from Botox® which basically every local dermatologist also provided. She understood that the more patients she could get in front of, the more of these additional services she could sell. She said the problem in her industry is that if a woman was already receiving Botox® elsewhere, they would have no reason to select her medical day spa instead of the place where they were getting Botox®.

I heard her say, "medical day spa." Instantly, I said, "You are different and unique." We then applied the Conversion Equation to her marketing to "convince" potential patients that they needed to go a "medical day spa" with a qualified doctor providing this service and not an esthetician. Our job was first to find women who were already getting Botox® and who were in the market for additional Botox® treatments and then compel them to leave their current estheticians and come to her "medical day spa." We did this with the Conversion Equation and established her Core Unique Positioning Statement®, which made her medical day spa the only logical choice.

We also brought in the upsell and cross-sell at the point of sale with her new patients. In her business, this was when her patients started their Botox® treatment with her. At the point of sale, she would instantly offer additional relevant products and services (cross-sell) and a Botox® package (upsell). She was able to not only increase the number of patients who came to her practice, within nine months' time, but she had also added over $188,500 to her income by ethically upselling and cross-selling, and her patients were delighted, too.

⑤ CASE STUDY-RESTAURANT ⑤

Because upselling and cross-selling are two critically important concepts, I will share another case study that illustrates how I have also put this in practice for a restaurant. I want to give a few different examples of these strategies in action so you can begin to see the possibilities and potential in your business.

Chef Rae, a client family member, owns a Thai restaurant. He hired me to help him increase his customer base and profits. I applied the Conversion Equation, and he quickly had more customers dining at his establishment. Then I helped to train his staff to offer every table an appetizer when they sat down and offer them a taste of red or white wine. These are his upsells. At least one of these offerings was accepted by over 50% of his patrons, and over 30% bought both, meaning they purchased an appetizer and a bottle of the wine they had tasted.

We didn't stop there. At the end of the meal, the waitstaff began to offer dessert without asking by bringing over the dessert tray to every table after the patrons finished their meal and before being offered tea or coffee. To make this offer work even better, I recommended that the waitstaff also leave a very small dessert sample on the table. After tasting the dessert and appreciating the restaurant's generosity, the restaurant sold three times as many desserts after implementing this strategy.

Later, we added one additional upsell strategy. We trained the servers to recommend each table when they were reviewing the menu and talking about the fresh fish sold at market value. The staff talked about how delicious the item is (it is!) and how popular it is and then personally said they would recommend this item. The item is, in fact, the most expensive item on the menu and delicious as well. The result? Over 17% of his patrons went with the wait staff's suggestion. This increased the average dinner ticket by over $13% also.

Upselling and cross-selling are sitting in every business. You are just not a trained expert at identifying your business's hidden marketing assets.

My client family members increase their bottom lines by 30-50% using just this one hidden marketing concept. However, being extremely conservative, let's just say you have only a 10% increase in your business after implementing this idea. What is 10% of your current annual revenue? That is what you could add to the bottom line of your business immediately using this strategy.

More Transactions by Expanding Product/Service Offerings

Here is another hidden marketing concept for increasing transactions: I help my client family members expand the number of products and services they offer.

Your business most likely has satisfied customers who are already thrilled with your products and services. These people already know, like, and trust you and your business. They will be likely to purchase additional products and services from your business due to their relationship with your business. I am shocked by how most businesses do not have additional products or services to offer their customer base. I am talking here about things you might not typically offer, not your core offerings.

One of my client family members is a business advisor specializing in off-line marketing through print ads. I asked him to make a list of other types of ads that might be needed by his customers that he did not provide. He put Facebook ads and pay-per-click ads on the list. I asked him if that would be valuable to offer to his customers. We agreed the answer was a resounding "yes." He did not have expertise to create these ads and no desire or time to learn how to do on-line ads. I connected him with another client family member of mine who specializes in on-line ads. Now he offers his off-line marketing print ad service as well as on-line marketing services to his customers and gets a referral or affiliate fee from each customer he refers to the on-line marketing expert. He is not only providing a greater service that his customer base needs, he is adding more income right to his bottom line and doing no extra work and all with zero cost.

⑤ CASE STUDY—LANDSCAPE HAND-WEEDING SPECIALIST ⑤

My client family member, Marta, specializes in the hand weeding of large personal properties. She truly does a phenomenal job, and her customers are thrilled with her work. When she hired me for business and marketing consulting, I asked if she saw any needs that her customers' outdoor areas may have. She created a list of potential ideas including landscaping, tree trimming, outdoor lights, pavers, outdoor patios, outdoor kitchens, fencing, swimming pools, hot tubs, sprinkler systems, and more. She did not provide any of these services and only wanted to be in the business of her expertise, which set her apart from all local weeding services. Her distinction in your niche was the fact her company weeded with no chemicals and that all weeding was done by hand.

I pointed out to her that she was in a unique position to make professional recommendations to her customers, and through this hidden marketing asset, she could not only make more income in less time, she could create even greater value for her customers. Together we agreed that most of her homeowners would be thrilled to have her recommendations to improve their outdoor properties as they already trusted her. I asked her to establish referral fees with these businesses. She set up four of these arrangements with people she trusted to deliver quality work and high value to her current customers. She received from 10% to 25% of each service.

Over the course of one year, she doubled her annual revenue by using this hidden marketing asset.

◎ CASE STUDY—LEADERSHIP TRAINER ◎

James, a client family member, works with his clients training them to become better leaders. I asked what else he could offer through affiliate or referral relationships. He told me he could offer a 360 assessment, DiSC® assessment, Myers-Briggs Type Indicator®, and speaker training. Since these were not his areas of expertise, he went about finding providers of these services. He found people who were highly skilled in these areas and who came with great recommendations and endorsements. He then began offering various assessments to his clients when they signed on with him and his revenue increased by over 50% in less than five months!

How many additional offerings do you estimate you could be making right now? All you need to do is contact each potential service provider you identify and effectively negotiate a deal with them that's a win-win-win. I would conservatively estimate that this strategy will add 10% to 50% in total revenue to your bottom line. It is just one of the many hidden marketing techniques I use to help business owners make more money in less time. Let's explore another hidden marketing asset now.

Bundling

Another way to increase your profits is to make higher-priced offerings when you sell your products or services. I recommend you do this through a concept called *bundling*. Bundling is the process of grouping together certain products or services and creating "packages" you then offer to your customers.

When you use this strategy, you completely remove the biggest complaint small business owners have these days: they are always competing on price. Bundling removes price from the equation. It works with your Core Unique Positioning Statement® by creating an "apples to oranges" comparison and taking away any "apples to apples" comparisons potential prospects may make.

All prospects shop for value and not for price. Yet, small business owners are not professional marketers, so they are not experts at creating or conveying their Core Unique Positioning Statement® or at *implementing* the Conversion Equation. Because of this, price is the only value proposition left to potential consumers.

The key to success in marketing is to offer more value than your competition. Your prospects, just like the prospects of my client family members, will pay twice the price if they believe they are receiving four times more value. Sadly, most businesses really do not know how to express or differentiate their value, so they offer reduced prices instead. This seriously cuts into their profit margins. In many instances, a business that discounts their price by a mere 10%, now has to sell 50% more products or services just to break even. This is a strategy that can put you right out of business.

Example

Let me illustrate this for you. Let's say I sell a $100 selfie-stick, and my profit margin is 20%. My business would make $20 for each selfie-stick sold. My cost basis would be $80. Since I do not have a Core Unique Positioning Statement®, and I never even heard of the Conversion Equation, and I have not invested in professional marketing help, my business is struggling to get prospects and to make a decent profit. I do not know what to do so I believe discounting my selfie-stick will bring more buyers. I decide to discount a mere 10% believing this will help my business. Instead of selling the product for $100, I reduce the price to $90. My cost base has not changed, and it remains at $80. Now I am only making $10 profit instead of the $20 profit I made before I reduced the price.

For this business to make $1,000 in profits selling their sticks, it would need to sell 50 of them. By discounting the price by only 10%, now the business will need to sell 100 of the sticks. That is double the amount of these items to only get back to their original profit margin. Instead of making more profit, the business would be losing out and in fact, may potentially be out of business with this strategy.

In truth, I rarely even see a business that uses only a 10% discount. Do you? Most businesses that hire me have given away 25% and up to 50% discounts prior to consulting with me! They do not understand why they are failing, and they also do not know that most prospects are not compelled to buy because of a discount.

The Conversion Equation, along with your Core Unique Positioning Statement® and the help of a qualified marketing professional, will ensure your business is built on creativity and innovation. You will be providing more value than your competitors and, in many cases, actually increasing your price and not decreasing your fees.

Bundling is the right way to increase the perceived value of your products and services. This system allows you to raise your fees and also to have your prospects buy more. It is one of the best, hidden marketing assets your business has.

Increase Prices

It makes sense to talk about increasing your prices as our next hidden marketing asset concept. Most business owners never even think to do this, and some are scared to do this because they fear losing their customers.

I recall when I just began in my consulting business, and I was fully booked with client family members in 30 days, I thought about increasing my fees. I felt I could do this because I created huge value and return on investment for my client family members. Yet, I was afraid all of my client family members would leave if I even raised my fees by a mere 10%. Then I did the math.

At the time, I was offering a consulting session for $250 per hour. I wanted to raise my fees by only $25 per consulting session. I realized my client family members were happy and logically didn't believe any would leave. Then I looked at what my business would look with the higher consulting fees.

I was charging $250 per session and keeping $200 of pure profit. If I increased my fees to $275 per session, I was now going to keep $225 dollars of profit. At my current fee of $250 per consulting session, I had to do five hours of sessions to make $1,000. If I were to increase my fees to $275 per session, I would only need to do 4.4 hours of consulting sessions. I would be doing fewer sessions, and I would have more free time. At the time when I considered raising my prices, I had 30 client family members and was earning $7500 per month and keeping $6000 in profits in my first few months as a start-up consulting business.

I did the math and realized that if I lost 10% of my current client family members when I raised my fees, which meant I would lose 3 of my 30 client family members, I would have billed $8250 for the month and would have earned profits of $6075 and I would be working 3 fewer hours each month while making more money. I realized I could afford to lose 3 client family members. If they did not see the value of working with me, I would prefer 3 other client family members who did see my value and were willing to invest just a tiny bit more to have my small business marketing consulting services.

Then I discovered that I could afford to lose 6 client family members, which I knew would not happen, and still break-even working 6 fewer hours!

That was my wake-up call.

There simply is no quicker, easier, and more effective way to generate additional revenue and profits than raising your prices. Do the math in your business right now!

Decrease Costs

The reverse way of increasing profits is to decrease the costs you currently have of doing business. This is another one of the hidden marketing assets your business may have. Most businesses have full-time employees, part-time employees, or independent contractors working with them. This is the largest expense a business owner typically has.

When I started my consulting business, I no longer wanted employees because of the expense in salary, taxes, benefits, unemployment, worker's comp, etc. And yet, I needed some help with tasks like accounting, email, client family member support, websites, and then later with social media, SEO, blogging, podcasting, and more. Initially, I bartered with my first virtual assistant. I helped her grow her own virtual consulting agency as her business and marketing consultant, and she was the virtual assistant in my business.

As my business grew, I had added many business and marketing consultants to my team, and I also needed to hire a large support team for the consultants who were also working with my client family members alongside me.

I decided that all the consultants and the support team would be brought on as independent contractors. At that time, I went to a local junior college and offered an internship to one of their students. I would work with the student who was studying business or marketing, and I would mentor them. In turn, for a semester, they would do tasks I needed in my company for no fee. I would write them a great letter of reference when they completed the internship. I applied the same internship strategy a few years later, when I started doing live workshops and seminars. I wanted to film my events professionally, but instead of paying thousands of dollars to have this done, I went to a local college and gave students who were studying film internships. So, my support team was "staffed" by interns at no cost.

To this day, I have student interns. I have two currently from Ithaca College, one of my alma maters. One does a lot of blogging and article writing, and the other is doing many research projects. I love working with the interns and find them full of new and creative ideas. They are innovators! They enjoy getting mentored by me as well. And the colleges love the fact that students can learn skills outside the classroom in a real work environment.

My interns are virtual today. In the past, I also had interns in my office and at my seminars and workshops. In fact, one of the students who was an intern with me two years ago got a much higher paid job than most of his class due to the real live work experience he had. Another intern who was on my team last year got so excited about the work we were doing that he decided to be an entrepreneur. He said I inspired him to start his own business and not apply for a job. Today he has his own very successful social media agency.

Add Them Up

Take a minute and add up a 10% price increase and the resulting profits plus a 10% decrease in monthly expenses. If you don't have any employees or independent contractors right now, you know you will in the future, so this is an immediate saving in any case.

Now go back to all the hidden marketing concepts covered in this chapter. Write down the additional revenues and profits you will gain if you only increase each area a meager 10%. So that you know, most of our client family members increase each area by 20-50% on average so we are super conservative in our estimates. And I have only revealed a very, very small sampling of hidden marketing assets I know we can find in your business.

Remember, I guarantee a start-up has $10,000 of hidden marketing assets and an established business has a minimum of $100,000 in hidden marketing assets. My team at Heartrepreneur LLC are experts at finding these assets in small businesses this is why we make this guarantee.

By applying hidden marketing assets to your business, you will generate additional revenue this year. You will be generating this additional revenue every year for your business's life.

⑤ CASE STUDY—PERSONAL TRAINER ⑤

My client family member, Richard, is a personal trainer. We increased his qualified prospects, conversions, transactions, and prices by only 10% in our first few months together. Prior to hiring me, he was averaging 52 leads per month and converting 30% of those leads into 16 paid clients a month. His clients averaged two personal training sessions a month at a fee of $125 per session. That gave Richard monthly revenues of $3,900. He had a relatively high 58% profit margin because he came to people's homes and did not have a brick and mortar gym.

Richard was only earning $2262 per month in gross profits. He had no idea what to do or how to grow his start-up business. He was frustrated and tired of struggling so he hired me to help him grow his business. He knew that $2262 per month would eat up the rest of his 401k and he would have to shut his doors unless he had my professional business consulting advice.

During his first month of my consulting services, we increased his leads to 57 per month using Guerrilla Marketing proven no-cost strategies to get more qualified prospects and applied the Conversion Equation. Conversions went up to 33%, and he now had 19 clients sign on with him over a one-month period. The personal training clients still averaged 2 sessions per week but now the fee per session was increased to $137.50. His revenue went from $3900 the prior month to $5710 the next month. More importantly, while he had a high-profit margin to begin with at 58% but only gross profits of $2262 when he started with me, we decreased his costs 10%. Now his gross profit margin was 63.8%. His gross profits were up almost double! He pocketed $4083 instead of $2262.

Let's see what happened in month four of our consulting work. By following the Conversion Equation and the concepts in this book, adding more proven tactics to his marketing, and refining his Core Unique Positioning Statement*, his leads went up to 78 leads per month with no added expenses used to generate those leads. Conversions went to up to 35% as the prospects he was getting were much more qualified. We also added the additional offering of a third personal training session and bundled this in his packaging and pricing because he felt a third weekly session would not only increase the number of transactions per client, more importantly, he wanted his clients to get the results they really wanted for their bodies. We bundled 3 sessions into packages, which raised his fees to $187.50 per session. Prior to working with me, he had 4 leads/month and was making about $4,000 a month. He now is doing about $30,000 average a month.

Remember, when he started with me in month one and his revenues were only $3900? Now, in just 4 months of consulting with me, his monthly revenue was at $19,744! I also got him higher gross profits by cutting even more costs from his marketing and advertising. The first month when he hired me, he only had $2262 in gross profit, and he was worried about going out of business, as you recall. This fourth month he lost all fear of going out of business. His gross profit was $19,250, and he could see the potential of adding more trainers and increasing his profits ten-fold.

His business skyrocketed to a quarter of a million annually in our first year together!

Your Business

Now let's look at your business. What if you got 10% more leads and 10% more conversions resulting in 10% more customers? What if you also increased your customer transactions by 10%, revenue, and profits by 10% and had 10% more gross profit?

Do the math. Then remember most of our client family members gain from 20-50% increases in each of these areas.

Let's do the math again using a 50% increase in each area, and you will quickly see this is how we use a precise formula to create six-, seven-, and even eight-figure businesses. When you have the right Core Unique Positioning Statement® and effectively apply the Conversion Equation, with Guerrilla Marketing, and the hidden marketing concepts in this chapter, with the best professional marketer on your team, you will generate a large number of qualified prospects. You'll also experience a higher conversion rate and additional sales— consistently across the board.

Your business will run on a systemized approach that is proven. And this system will bring you not only more incredible wealth, it will also give you more freedom of time. Instead of constantly hunting for customers, you will have proven strategies in place filling your pipeline with qualified prospects. You will have effective, proven low and zero-cost Guerrilla Marketing working for you every day.

Besides, you will have joint ventures and affiliate partners and strategic alliances with your customers setting the stage for additional prospects and income. You will have up-sells, down-sells, and cross-sells taking place every day and you will be providing logical additional affiliate products and services to your customers. Your fees will go up and your customers will happily pay your new fees due to your businesses' higher perceived value. And finally, you will have lower costs and huge amounts of additional revenue and profits.

CHAPTER 9
MORE LEADS—THE SECRETS THAT WORK

T he most often overlooked hidden marketing asset of a company is their existing customer base. This base consists of your former, current, and prospective customers. While most business owners are hunting for cold prospects and spending a lot of time and money to do so, your customer base is where to generate leads and make more profits fast.

I always tell my client family members that I want them to keep their customers for life instead of hunting to find more qualified prospects. I ask them—and am now asking you—to put your focus on your own existing customer database.

$ CASE STUDY—IT CONSULTING FIRM $

Let me illustrate how effective this strategy is. Jim, a client family member, owns an IT consulting firm and has been in business for over six years. He hired me because he wanted to grow his business. He had been using SEO, pay-per-click, and Facebook ads, as well as direct mail. They were all wasting his time, energy, and money with lackluster results. I asked if he had an existing database. Having been in business nearly a decade he told me he had an email list in a contact relationship manager (CRM) software, he used to send them newsletters.

He had over 1500 people's email addresses of various businesses he had serviced over the years.

Instead of sending out his regular newsletter, I helped him craft an email to send to everyone on his database, offering new services. Just one email generated over $16,000 in revenue. Literally, in less than 7 days, he added $16,000 in revenue to his business.

Your Database

No matter the size, I believe your database is gold in your business and is filled with untapped lead generation potential. Why? Statistics show that 65% of people stop doing business with a company because they feel unimportant to that company. If customers feel a company is apathetic towards them, they leave. Catch my point.

Contrary to popular belief, most customers do not leave due to price, quality, or selection. The primary reason customers stop doing business with a company is that they stop feeling important to that company.

When I am making a purchase, I want to feel special. Then when I become a customer, if I am not feeling special anymore, I go elsewhere. This is normal human behavior. Become aware of your current customer base being your biggest source of qualified prospects to buy from you. You will have the secret to how I build multi-million-dollar companies over and over again with ease, provided you have a CRM.

I am often amazed that many businesses do not have a CRM. They have emails or invoices or scattered data, and that data is often missing essential information. You must have a CRM that has the customer's name, snail mail address, phone number, email address, along with their purchasing history of what they bought and for what prices and how they heard of your company or where they opted in from.

If you do not have this information today, that is okay. I want you to begin today by getting a CRM like ActiveCampaign, Hubspot, Insightly, MailChimp®, Constant Contact®, or Zoho. If you have any email addresses or receipts of transactions from past customers, current customers and even prospective customers can immediately put them into your CRM with the information I mentioned is necessary.

To consistently have people added to your CRM, you will attach the CRM to your websites, landing pages or opt-in pages. Suppose you own a brick and mortar business. In that case, you can enter receipts into the CRM daily or can have a drawing or contest that customers and prospective customers can enter by providing their names, snail mail addresses, phone numbers, and email addresses. Also, be sure to ask how they heard of your business.

As you advance with your use of a CRM or if you currently have a CRM, you might want to add information on birthdays, anniversaries, information about your customer's families, and their hobbies. The better you know your customers personally, the more you can be in touch with your customers. When customers feel you care about them and want them as customers for life, the more loyal they will become.

⑤ CASE STUDY—HAIR SALON OWNER ⑤

My client family member, Jill, owns a hair salon. She hired me to bring her business more qualified prospects and more income as she wanted to sell her business in a few years and wanted her business valuation to be higher. I looked at her database, and she had over 1500 customers who had purchased from her salon since its inception. She thought I was going to help her get qualified prospects by marketing to a cold audience. I said that was the "hard" way and I'd like to have her do it the "easy" way. She was in!

The first thing we did was communicate with her customer base. She had captured their names, snail mail addresses, phone numbers, and what they purchased from her salon. Her communication with them up until hiring me had been to send a 15% off postcard by snail mail once a year. She also sent her customers her salon's magazine by email quarterly, and there was a special coupon in the magazine offering a 15% discount each quarter, too. She also knew through her CRM, only 10% of all the postcards she sent were redeemed and that only 9% of the emails with the magazine ever got opened and most coupons in the magazine were never even seen.

I shared two strategies with her, and I implemented them both in her business. These strategies are called *reactivation* and *recall*. Let's look at reactivation first.

Reactivation is a very simple and effortless strategy that most businesses are missing out on. It is a major secret to generating prospects. The goal is to reactivate past customers who are no longer buying from your business for whatever reason. Think about this. You have a customer's contact information, and you already have a relationship with them as a buyer. It makes sense to touch them and to be in contact with them. You will reach out to touch base with them to reactivate them, and you will give these customers a special or a discount to show them that your business cares and truly wants to serve them.

Back to Jill's business. I first had her gather data on which customers had stopped coming to her salon. These customers may have changed hair salons for a number of reasons. Maybe they moved or they didn't feel nurtured, embraced, or special at her salon. If you lose a customer, you most likely do so because your business does not have a systemized way of keeping in touch with them and showing them how important they are to your business and how much you want to keep them as lifetime customers.

I asked Jill to have her salon receptionist pull up all the customers in her database who had not purchased in over a year. Then I helped Jill craft a heartfelt letter telling her former customers that she missed them and enjoyed having them as a customer and was grateful to have served them. She also added that her salon would love to serve them again. She then asked them why they left, and if she or her staff had done anything that offended them, or if the salon had not served them fully. She told them that she was prepared to do everything in her power to make it right.

We sent that letter by snail mail and by email and a very special, highly discounted, limited offer to get them back to her shop. She gave her cell phone number and her private email to them instead of the salon's email and invited them to contact her if they had any problem in their experience with the salon. She told them she promised to personally listen to them and do her best to make it right.

Additionally, I helped her train her two front desk receptionists to implement a recall strategy. Customers who came in on occasion and were not steady but who might come for a cut or color every few months or every few years and were not considered "regulars" withstanding appointments went on the recall list. I had her receptionists personally call each of these customers to recall them and make them a special offer to come in for a cut and color at 50%.

We systematized both the reactivation and recall strategies so that the CRM system would trigger who needed to be recalled and who needed to be reactivated. As this salon used both the reactivation and recall strategies that I helped them create and implement, Jill added over $105,000 in revenues to her salon within less than six months.

Business by Referral

The other secret lead generating system I am sharing is based on building your business by referral. Most businesses don't get as many qualified prospects as they want or need because they rarely communicate with their customers. I communicate often. If you are on my email list you already know I send a valuable tip or tool to you ever single week. You must communicate with your customers often, so they feel you care.

Your job is to build long-term relationships with your customers. If you do this right, not only will your customers stay with you because they will feel important to your business, they will refer more qualified prospects to you. This is the essence of relationship marketing and how I have built all of my business and turned them into referral-based businesses.

Learn these words: Capture, Care, Communicate, and Reward.

You must *capture* the customer and prospective customer information for your CRM. Then you must show you *care* about your customers and prospects by communicating with them regularly and not pitching them, and finally, you must reward them for referrals. Suppose you are not constantly adding value with your customer and prospective customer *communications. In that case,* they will stop buying or will not consider buying, and they certainly will not be inclined to refer their family and friends to your business. Then reward them for being loyal customers and referring new prospects to you.

Look at my example of this *not* happening.

Recently, I downloaded an SEO checklist. Within minutes I had four sales emails from the person who created the checklist. I went from being a potential buyer of his services to unsubscribing. He captured my information, and then he did not show me he cared about me, and his communication was not of value, so not only did I unsubscribe, I told others not to bother with him.

Imagine if he did this, right?

Here is an example of how I interacted with a recent Instagram expert and how his communication got me to hire him.

This expert found me on Instagram, and he offered me his service. Before he even asked me to hire him, he said he wanted to first demonstrate his value by creating a video for my Instagram account. I was thrilled. Sure, I'll take a professionally done free video. I gave him all my contact information, which he captured. When he sent me the video, it had one very minor error, and I pointed it out. Keep in mind he created the video for free. He quickly re-did the video. I was not expecting this at all. I felt he cared. He then communicated with me by sending me a 30-second video telling me how much he wanted to work with me. He communicated. I hired him and was thrilled with his service. He asked if I knew other influencers. I named a few, and then I contacted them and referred them to do business together. As a reward, he added five free videos to my service!

You must be consistently capturing data, showing you care, providing authentic communication and rewarding your customers for referring business to you.

You will find when you implement these strategies in your business, your customers will invest in your products or services and spend more money with you than ever before—and you will turn on a referral engine.

⑤ CASE STUDY-COPYWRITER ⑤

Martha is a client family member who creates courses, and she also does copywriting. She hired me because she wanted more prospects and more income. She did not have a CRM as she was a newer business and did not think she needed one. I had her upload the data she had about her customers and prospects from the Excel file, where she had been keeping this information to a free CRM tool.

Once that was done, I helped Martha implement reactivation and recall strategies with the small database she already had. I then went on to apply my system of capture, care, communicate, and reward to her business. We set up a frequent buyer program for her best customers, along with a referral reward program as part of this system. All of her top customers were sent a discount on their next course or copywriting project.

I am certain you are aware of the saying that it costs a lot less to keep a current customer than to acquire a new one, right? I am always fascinated that while most business owners know this, they still spend most of their marketing time and money acquiring new customers. This is what Martha had been doing. I told her—and I will tell you—that your current customers are the foundation of your business.

Martha and I created an incentive for her loyal customers where for each dollar they spent with her, they would get "Martha Money" which we printed inexpensively on something that looked like a dollar bill. If they spent $400, they got $400 "dollars" in "Martha Money." The dollars could be redeemed for gifts. The gifts ranged from books, courses, and programs, to iPads. The more they spent, the more they got rewarded.

Next, we focused on leveraging her current customer base to gain more qualified prospects and increase her profits and revenues through referrals. In my experience, most businesses do not have a systematic way of getting referrals from satisfied customers. Putting this system in place in her business resulted in colossal rewards.

First, I had her set up regular valued email tips that she then sent to her database weekly. Every fourth email would remind her customers that referrals were the lifeblood of her business. Those referrals allowed her to spend time focused on creating courses and copywriting for her customers instead of hunting for more customers. She talked about wanting to be with her customers for the life of their businesses. In these emails, she reminded her database that she gave special rewards for giving her business referrals. She not only gave a reward to her current customer she also gave a reward to any friends, family, or colleagues they referred to her business.

As a result of the reward program, she generated 10 qualified prospects with only one email! Keep in mind that she had a small database and had not been an established business for a long time. Remember the endorsement letters I talked about earlier? Well, we decided also to use letter of endorsement because they not only work; they are one of my favorite lead generation techniques.

If I want more prospects at any given time in my business, I can usually increase prospects at least ten-fold by implementing this simple idea. I have zero-cost with this strategy, too. So, I love it, and I use it with most of my client family members.

I also asked Martha to simply identify one company she knew of that had a product or service and an existing customer base in a CRM that aligned with her course creation or copywriting. I asked her to provide her course or her copywriting to that company for free in exchange for a letter of endorsement.

Let me make a clear distinction here. I was not asking her to gather a testimonial. In this case, a letter of endorsement is when the business she provides the free valuable product or service to happily tells their entire database about their experience with her product or program and endorses her business.

Early on in my consulting business, I gave a very big-name influencer, coach, and author access to my health and wellness consulting program for free as he wanted to lose weight. I only had 400 email subscribers at that time, and he had thousands. He loved my program, and he lost 20 pounds in under six weeks without dieting or exercise. We agreed that if my program worked, he would write a letter of endorsement and send this to his database. His database could certainly use my services and products, and his business specialized something very different than weight loss help.

I wanted to increase my database and brand recognition and enroll more prospects into my weight loss consulting program and my other life and business consulting services. And I did not want to spend my time, money and energy hunting for prospects. I crafted the endorsement letter for him. Why? I wanted to be sure it would be written in a way that truly endorsed my program. Then I sent the letter to him to approve or tweak and to send it to his database.

The letter talked about how he had been carrying around 20 pounds of weight for three years and that he hated dieting and exercise, yet knew he needed to lose weight for health purposes. It went on to talk about my program and how in less than six weeks he easily shed the weight without dieting or exercise and how thrilled he was with the results. The letter then suggested he thought this would of interest to his clients, and he mentioned that I was gifting a free e-book about weight loss to all his clients. He said he arranged for me to give that book away to his valued customers only. This was all true.

We included a link where they could enter their names and email addresses to get their free ebook so that I could do lead capture and build a database of prospects. The letter ended with my client telling his readers how valuable the gift was for them and how delighted he was to have been able to arrange this for them.

Overnight, my email list grew to over 55,000 subscribers. I also enrolled 1500 of those people into my weight loss consulting program in just four days at an investment of $1297 each. The total cost to me was zero, and my earnings were $1,945,500 in four days! And, many of these subscribers later purchased other programs and products from me. Those people who did enroll in my weight loss course also made additional purchases over the years.

CHAPTER 10
MORE CONVERSIONS--WITH EASE

I have shown you an easy and effortless process to attract qualified prospects to your business. Now it is time to convert them into paying customers quickly. Let me first state that I am not a fan of using sales or manipulation tactics or overcoming objections to have customers purchase. I help my client family members learn how to *Sell Without Selling* (https://www.amazon.com/Sell-Without-Selling-Lessons-Success/dp/1600374646) based on my bestselling book. Like me, I have my client family members only spend time with high-quality prospects and help those prospects to decide to invest in their products and services.

Before I show you how to convert qualified prospects into paying customers, you must know how to identify highly qualified prospects. Otherwise, you will waste a lot of time with prospects who never intend to invest in your services. You must sort your prospects to discover who is serious about investing in your products and services and who would be an ideal customer for you.

Time is a precious commodity. It is something we can never get back, and life is going by every single day, so we have less time on the planet. I only want you to invest your time into serious prospects who are qualified buyers. I want to protect your time by not having you waste your time and your money!

The A, B, C, D System

In my first business, I learned to sort prospects using an *A, B, C, and D system*. I share this system with all my client family members, and you also need to learn this system. A prospect labeled "A" is hungry for your products and services and is considered a "now" buyer. "B" prospects are also interested in your products or services yet are not ready to purchase right now. This could be due to health, how busy they are, finances, etc. "C" prospects are serious about your prospects and services at some point. "C" prospects currently do not have a need or desire to invest with you, though. "D" prospects either have no desire ever to purchase your products or services.

To create a six-, seven-, and even eight-figure business, you must become an expert at sorting and sifting the "A's" from the rest. You can spot an "A" prospect by their desire for your products and services and the financial means to purchase right now. Keep in mind; not all prospects are rated equally. Not all of them truly need what you sell or are ideal for you to sell to. Also keep in mind that people buy what they want and not what they need.

I recently purchased a new sound system for our home. We did not need one. We had a decent one. Yet, I wanted a new one, and therefore I made a purchase. There are things I need but do not want, and I ignore those products and services until they may someday show up as a want.

As another example, my husband needs shoulder surgery. He has known this for over five years. So why doesn't he have it? He isn't ready. It is not a want for him. He isn't ready for the rehabilitation and physical therapy that he will undergo due to the surgery.

Unless a prospect has a very have a strong want, they are not an "A" prospect for you and are not considered a qualified prospect. Qualified prospects are ready to buy now and have the funds to invest in your products and services. If you are like many of my client family members when they first start consulting with me, you may be spending your time trying to sell to the wrong people and scratching your head, wondering why so few of them convert into paying customers. This could also be because you have not clearly defined and verified that the niche you have chosen to focus on actually, generally speaking, has the funds to pay for your products or services. Simply put, you cannot convert a prospect who doesn't have the funds to buy from you. "A" prospects have access to the funds.

Lastly, there is one more qualification that a prospect needs to have to be considered "A." That is that they must be the decision-maker for the purchase of your products or services. In my business, I am the decision-maker for all products and services in which I invest. Yet, many companies waste their time scheduling meetings with other people on my team. They are speaking with someone who has no ability to decide to buy their products and services and are wasting their time as well as my team member's time.

What if a prospect wants what you sell, and they do have the ability to purchase and are not the decision-maker? For me, they become a "B" prospect. They are a "C" prospect if they only meet one criterion, like having the authority to purchase but not the funds to purchase as an example. The remaining prospects are of no interest to us, and you need to let them go.

Focus

Almost all business owners focus their marketing on the wrong things. You will be successful at marketing because I am showing you how to focus on the real reason customers buy from you. They buy from your business because your business helps them solve something they are dealing with in business or life that is a problem area for them. Then your product or service helps them overcome their problem or achieve their goals. Your competitors will be focused on credentials, education, awards, and achievements. These are not the reasons a prospect will purchase from your company.

Remember that your prospects don't care about your credentials. They buy from your business because of your reputation and your Core Unique Positioning Statement® that demonstrates you understand their situation and can bring them the results they want. The Conversion Equation brought them to you, and they see your business as the only logical choice who understands them and has a solution to their problem. They want results and want your business to deliver the results they desire.

I learned that these things are not important and then created this proprietary CUPS formula. When I first started in the coaching and consulting space. I told prospects about all my degrees and certifications and credentials and licenses I held. Then, General Electric hired me. I asked them why me they selected me. I believed it was because of my degrees. They told me that I was the only one who understood their issue and guaranteed the result they wanted.

That was a great lesson. I realized the only thing a qualified prospect cares about is that your product or service can solve their problem and provide them with a guaranteed solution for their problem. That is the purpose of the Conversion Equation and of creating a Core Unique Positioning Statement® (CUPS).

Creating Your Core Unique Positioning Statement®

I have eluded to Core Unique Positioning Statement® (CUPS), dropping hints about it throughout the book. Finally, it is time to reveal what this is and exactly how to craft it! I just said your credentials, training, and degrees are not so special.

The typical business owner will create a "unique selling proposition" or an "elevator pitch". They might say something like this, "I help you go from point A to point B really fast," or "I turn dreams into reality" as examples. These statements say nothing about what a qualified prospect's pain is or the problem or pain these businesses' products or services solve. They are filled with jargon and do not make the company stand out to be the ONLY business a prospective customer can choose.

I am certain you have heard statements like the above at networking groups or even seen them or heard them on social media and in both on-line and off-line ads. My proprietary CUPS technique is built by first saying something like "I help,", "I serve," "I solve," or "We help," "We serve," or "We solve." Notice we don't start with the fact you are a coach, chiropractor, attorney, dentist or other professional. Your title or the name of your company has no value and no relevance and does not answer "what's in it for me" which is the question in a prospect's mind.

Your CUPS will say very specifically who you help so that the statement will interrupt the right target audience. Instead of saying I help women, for example, you will target the small niche of women you specifically want to attract with your marketing. Your CUPS might say, "I serve single women between the ages of 20-35," or "We help women ages 30-50 who are thinking about starting a home-based business."

Next, we have to tell the exact result we deliver to the prospects we have interrupted. We must keep them engaged by telling them about the result our business generates that stands apart from every other business in our industry.

In my business, as an example, my CUPS is, "I help small business owners who are struggling to find more qualified prospects to have a conveyor belt of qualified prospects..." I have interrupted my target audience of struggling business owners who want more qualified prospects to get the result they desire and keep them engaged by talking about the solution they desire, a conveyor belt of qualified prospects.

Now, my CUPS statement makes me the only choice as I mention something proprietary. "I help small business owners who are struggling to find more qualified prospects to have a conveyor belt of qualified prospects using my proprietary HEART® method." No one else can have or can use the HEART® method as I created and developed this. I am the only small business marketing consultant with this method.

So far, my CUPS has interrupted the right prospects, kept them engaged, and showed them I am the one and only best choice. Finally, a CUPS ends with the word "guaranteed." Here is my CUPS: "I help small business owners who are struggling to find more qualified prospects to have a conveyor belt of qualified prospects using my proprietary HEART® method—guaranteed."

I firmly believe if your business cannot or is not willing to stand behind your products and services, you should not be in business. My guarantee clearly positions me as my prospects only logical choice if they are a small business owner struggling to get more qualified prospects. In fact, in my twenty-five plus years as a marketing consultant I cannot find any other marketing consultant or business consultant who is willing to guarantee a potential 200% return on investment. If I fail to achieve results, I give back their entire consulting investment plus I pay them $5,000 for wasting their time!

Keep in mind that everything you do and say in your marketing must focus on solving problems that you know your ideal prospects have and guaranteeing them results. Your CUPS must be formatted the way I just taught you because it will do all the work of engaging and interrupting—and will position your business as the clear choice for your prospective customers.

While I help my client family members earn a lot more money, I also help them create a lot more freedom in their lives. I assist them in:

- developing an effective CUPS,
- sorting out the prospects who are not their target audience,
- sifting out those who are not interested in the results they deliver because they do not have the pain or struggle or frustration their business solves, and
- separating only the qualified "A" prospects who have the problem, want the proprietary solution, and the guarantee appeals to them.

I do not want my client family members or you to be spending time with prospects that are not serious and do not meet the criteria we just discussed above. I want you to spend less time dancing with people who don't want to be your dance partner and more time with people who do!

When you create the right CUPS, you will have your target market identify themselves with this reverse marketing strategy, where they will approach your business instead of your business approaching them. Your focus will shift from trying to sell to all prospects to only talking with qualified "A" prospects who have the desire, authority, and funds to purchase your products and services. This will transform your entire business.

Example

In our business, prospects attend our training after reading or hearing our CUPS. They have been interrupted and engaged, and now we provide them with free education by watching a training session.

After my training I offer a Profit Acceleration Session (www.tlwebinar.com/blueprint) to prospects. At Heartrepreneur LLC (www.heartrepreneur.com), we want to speak to "A" prospects only. Instead of offering free sessions, like most business and marketing consultants do, and spending most of their time with unqualified prospects, we have prospects complete an application and invest in this session. These prospects are accepting our zero-risk offer where we guarantee we will find $10,000 in hidden marketing assets if they are a start-up or $100,000 or more in hidden marketing assets if they are an established business guaranteed or we cheerfully refund their money if we fail to do so.

Notice all of the elements of the Conversion Equation are being used in this example.

Based on my CUPS and the CUPS format I shared with you, it is time for you to create your own CUPS. Once you do this, you must integrate your CUPS everywhere in all your marketing and advertising, including your website, social media headers, email signature file, business card, etc..

With the right CUPS created and implemented. You will be able to attract more qualified prospects.

"A" Prospects Only

From this moment on, I urge you to stop doing any type of free sessions, calls, assessments, demonstrations, always give, etc. I also encourage you only to speak with and to meet with actual decision-makers. If prospects do not have the authority to invest in your products and services, then there is no reason to spend time with them. Make this a firm policy in your business, and you will stop wasting your time. If for any reason a prospect does not agree with your terms, let them go, they are not good prospects for you anyway.

Before you schedule any calls, meetings, video chats, or anything else, you must determine whether this prospect is a qualified "A" prospect. Your prospects need to know your fees and have the funds to invest in what you are selling, and you need to know if you can solve the problem the prospect has.

I do this by having them complete an assessment before we take time for a call or a meeting, and I suggest you do the same thing. The assessment lets me know of a prospect's potential ability and desire to invest in my small business marketing consulting services and is a way for me to determine if I believe I can get the prospect of the results they desire. Since I offer a guarantee that is so unique in my CUPS, I must be confident I can give a prospect a guaranteed result.

One of my client family members, Leon Chan, is a business coach and before I helped him install this process in his business, he was spending ten hours or more weekly talking to prospects who were not ready or willing to invest in his coaching. Often the prospects he was speaking with wanted a result he could not provide. After we designed and implemented his CUPS, he told me that he created a screening assessment and understood "A" prospects. He saved hours every week talking to unqualified prospects, and he closed more prospects in less time, too.

I do not want you wasting your time doing anything that is not likely to bring you income. This is why everything I share with my client family members and here in the *Conversion Equation* has been tested with over 6,000 client family members in 444 different industries. It works.

Let your competitors do it wrong, while you do it right!

Consulting Questions

During your meeting with a qualified "A" prospect in person, by phone, or by video chat, you must take the lead. You do this by asking questions. Your job is to listen and not to fill the prospect with information. You will ask questions, and then you will deeply listen to your prospect's answers. Think of yourself as a consultant helping a prospect and not a salesperson trying to sell and close a prospect.

You will ask powerful coaching questions designed to find the prospect's problems and the result they desire. These questions are:

- If we were meeting a year from today, what would have had to happen for you to say our work together was successful?
- What is in your way of success?
- If you could have whatever you want in your business and your life, what is the ONE thing you want and are willing to commit to?

Spend most of the time in the meeting tuning in to your prospect's answers, with no attachment to closing a prospect. I suggest you watch my TedX talk (www. youtube.com/watch?v=2EhBPInXRyM) that will drive home this concept, too.

When you take on the role of being a consultant or coach in this sales process, you will not be the one doing most of the talking during these meetings. You do not need to talk a lot because your assessment has pre-qualified the prospect. You simply listen to prospects with your heart, and you hear the problems and the associated pain beneath their words. As you hear their problem, you assess if your products and services can help them.

If you believe you can help them, you share your CUPS and ask them to offer a solution to their problem. If you do not feel they are an "A" prospect, you do not offer your services or products. I recommend that you provide any prospects that are not qualified "A" prospects with some value during the meeting and then you part as friends.

Think about your most recent prospect calls. Can you see how much time you are wasting with prospects who are not qualified? This is why you do not close as many customers as you would like. My desire is to help you make more money, have more customers, experience less stress, and enjoy more free time, like me—and many of my client family members.

Follow-Up

When a prospect does not buy what you sell, do you follow up with them? Converting prospects into paying customers is not just about having one conversation with them. If you remember I told you earlier that less than 1% of prospects are ready to buy right now. This means that 99% of the prospects you will encounter are not prepared to purchase at the moment when you meet with them. They may be buyers down the road if you keep in touch with them and create value for them on an ongoing basis.

One of the problems I see with small business owners is that they focus all their efforts on creating leads. Then, if a lead does not convert to a sale, they hunt for another lead. They are continually seeking leads, and this can be exhausting, frustrating, and expensive as well.

I suggest that instead of focusing on getting more and more leads, you follow up with your prospects after your initial contact with them. Why? 80% of all sales are closed after 5-12 contacts with a prospect. If you are not doing some form of follow-up, you miss a big opportunity to close more prospects and create more income and end the constant customer hunting game.

Drip Campaign

It is essential to keep in touch with all prospects who meet your qualifications and who did not purchase yet. I like to do this by sending a video email (www. dubb.com/?ref=terrilevine1) message about our meeting and my desire to help them. I address their problem, re-state my solution and my guarantee, and remind them of my offer. This message is customized based on our conversation and is personal and from my heart.

Whether you do this by video or audio or the written word, you must remind them how your products or services can help them. You can also point them to video testimonials (www.tlwebinar.com) and case studies like I do.

Keep in mind that you are not trying to sell them or convince or manipulate them to buy from you or your company. You are just taking away any concerns they may have without overcoming any objections directly. Prospects can see and hear the proof of what other customers, just like them are saying. This can help alleviate any doubts and remind them you are here and would love to help them when and if they are ready.

The added credibility from my client family member testimonials removes any skepticism my prospects may have. My prospects watch real people sharing their own successes who have hired me as their small business and marketing consultant.

This is a powerful way to convert sales without selling and is part of my secret closing and "selling without selling" process. Sending my prospects, a link to the video testimonials is a powerful strategy, and when combined with my personal video email, many prospects close themselves quickly. Keep in mind people are skeptical by nature. This is why sometimes they will need to have more than one touchpoint to give them a level of comfort with your company.

I recommend that after you send the personalized email video and the link to your testimonials you begin an automated drip campaign. A drip campaign will close a lot of the prospects who were not immediately ready to purchase. Your CRM sends out this campaign and automatically sends a form of communication to prospects on a predetermined and scheduled basis. The drip campaign is not a sales pitch. Instead, you continuously educate and give value with a drip campaign. This can be a video email, email, or any other form of regularly scheduled automation.

⑤ CASE STUDY—PUBLISHING CONSULTANT ⑤

This client family member is a consultant who helps speakers, coaches, trainers, consultants, and others to self-publish books. There is a lot of confusion about what self-publishing means and how to do it. Because of this, I had her create a Consumer Awareness Guide as part of her drip campaign titled *The 5 Deadly Mistakes You Can Make in Self-Publishing That Will Waste Your Time and Money* and is sub-titled *Self-Publish the Easy Way: Sell More Books and Make More Money*. This is the first piece in her drip campaign and is sent four days after she has spoken with a prospect and after she has sent them her video email along with her video testimonial link.

After four additional days after this has gone out, her CRM automatically sends out another guide called an *Idea Guide for Self-Publishing*. Both guides are PDF files with great content and are of high value to her prospective client family members. The Consumer Awareness Guide teaches the mistakes her prospective clients must avoid when self-publishing and shows how her consulting can make self-publishing easy and profitable for her prospects. The Idea Guide talks about self-publishing benefits over traditional publishing and gives numerous tips and ideas to make a self-published book effective.

By implementing this drip campaign, she closed an additional 6 of every 10 prospects she had spoken to but did not initially purchase her services. Upon a few more touches, prospects decided on their own to invest in her self-publishing course or her self-publishing consulting. All of these customers enrolled directly as a result of her drip campaign.

And the campaign does not stop there. Every week she has another valuable educational tip or tool that she automates in her CRM to send to all prospects and her current customers.

Over a year, she has another 2 of the 10 people she initially spoke with purchase her course. Out of 10 prospects who do not purchase the first time, she is now closing 8 of them or 80%! She has maintained this closing ratio over three years now using this drip campaign sequence, which takes almost zero time to implement.

It's Your Turn

Being very conservative, how might this secret closing process I have shared with you impact your business? Keep in mind, 80% of sales take place after 5-12 touchpoints. Most of your competitors are sending out emails that contain no real value and, in fact, are sales pitches. They do not send out Consumer Awareness Guides or Education Guides.

Your business will stand out using this educational and valuable drip campaign strategy. You *will* see a significant increase in conversions and sales just like my client family members, and I do.

To give you an idea about how a drip campaign can add income to your business, let's start by looking at your total revenue from last year. Once you have that number, I want you to add a very conservative 10% conversion rate you would get from implementing my proven drip campaign strategy. This is a great way to see what a ridiculously low estimate of what a drip campaign can quickly and easily produce for your business over the next year. And this campaign can work to close sales and produce more income year after year after year. This is an exponential way to grow your business.

The Secret Sauce

I have a secret system I share with my client family members. It is comprised of two parts, and I will share both with you. One part is about the actual conversation to have with a prospect, and the other is a special follow-up report you send every prospect. Not only does this work, no one does this unless I have shown them my "secret sauce."

I will reveal this information to you in a moment.

Before I do, let me share one crucial element, which underlies this system. Even though I have trained over 1,000 salespeople and have worked as a sales trainer in major corporations and presented hundreds of keynotes and sales and a given TEDx talk on selling, I have never advocated using sales scripts. However, I do have two tools that make up my secret sauce. Together they make a massive difference for conversions. The system I am about to share with you allows you to have your prospects close themselves. I typically have over 82% of all "A" prospects say "yes" to me thanks to my secret sauce.

Ready for this bonus information?

Keep a few things in mind first. While I do not suggest you have a sales script, I do suggest you have a series of powerful questions ready to ask prospects. These questions follow the Conversion Equation. The questions are designed to point out the pain and emotional hot buttons of a prospect and help them decide to invest in your products or services to remove their problem. Once again, you are not agitating their pain. You are ethically pointing out the pain they are already dealing with.

I am going to give those questions to you now. Most business owners lack the knowledge of exactly what questions to ask, and they do not know what to say to a qualified prospect to help them decide to make a purchase.

So, do not worry about memorizing a script. Give up that idea completely. You want to listen and have these powerful questions in your mind. Do not read the questions. Instead, make the questions your own and ask them naturally.

Before you start asking questions, begin each meeting by explaining the purpose of the meeting to the prospect. Tell the prospect that your intention is to spend time together so you can find what their problem is and to assist them with their problem if you have a solution for them.

Let them know upfront you are not going to sell them. Keep in mind people do love to buy. However, they do not like to be sold, and they are typically on the alert for a sales pitch, which may make them defensive.

Give them comfort in letting them know right away that this is not a sales meeting. Then, tell your prospects that you will pay close attention and deeply listen to them—and that you will do your best to help them. Then you ask their permission to ask some questions.

Each question is designed to find their hot buttons and to evoke emotion. Once you have identified and felt their emotion underneath their problems, you can then guide your prospects as to how your product or service can solve their problem, if, in fact, it can. The questions' job is to engage your prospects and reveal that your services or products have the answers to the prospect's problems. You conclude all of your meetings by asking your prospects if they want your product or service if you have recommended it as a solution for them.

The Questions

Remember, these are not sales questions. These are coaching questions that help uncover a prospect's pain and guide a prospect to their answers. If you go into sales mode, prospects are likely to become defensive. You are not showing up to make a sale. You are showing up to help someone who has a problem. This is the right mentality you must have going into your meetings. This is what I refer to as "the selling without selling shift." When you concentrate on your prospect's needs and you care about them, prospects can make their own decisions without you selling them anything.

Opening Questions

Your opening questions are designed to solidify trust and rapport.

- I am here to help you overcome your problem, and I want to fully understand you and your problem and not sell you anything. Ok?
- Would it be ok if I ask you some questions since I am an expert at knowing if my product or service will help you?
- And do you understand that even if my product or service isn't right for you, I may have some suggestions?
- Ok?

Pain Questions

- What is the problem you are having that I can potentially solve or help you solve?

- I want you to help me experience your pain truly, so take me into your story to feel the problem with you, ok?

Solution Questions
- What has to happen for you to invest in a solution to your problem?

These are basic, simple, coaching questions designed to create a natural conversation and guide prospects to make their own decisions without you selling them anything. That's it!

Pretty simple, right? If you ask these questions and truly listen deeply to the prospect's emotions, it will be easy to follow the second part of my secret formula.

The Follow-Up Report

After each meeting, you will write a concise report. The purpose of the report is to show you understand the prospect's problem, and you have a product or service to remove their problem. In this brief report, you summarize their situation using the words they told you when they expressed their problem to you during the meeting. You will list how your product or service will solve their problem and then you will share the expected results they will have if they invest in your products or services.

Be certain the prospect needs your product or service to get the result they want and cannot achieve the result without your product or service. Bullet out the results and outcomes they will get when using your product or service and conclude the report by telling the prospect exactly what action they need to take now to move forward with their purchase.

I recommend that even if the prospect said "no" when you offered them your service or product in the meeting, if they were an "A" prospect, you still send them the report. Why? My experience with this system is that 1 of every 5 who say "no" at first will come back and purchase within a month of receiving the report.

Think about this: Even if they initially did not invest in your solution, they still have the problem and are always thinking of solving it, right? If your business has the solution, the report keeps your business top of mind for them. They might not be the 1% who is ready to purchase today, and you want their business if they decide to buy later.

Using this method of sending a report by email within 48 hours after each prospect meeting, your business will be differentiated from all your competitors. Title the piece, either "Customer Report," "Client Report," or "Patient Report," depending on your business. The report's title shows them you already are considering them as a customer and that you want to help them overcome their problem. Sending these reports will create tremendous results for you in differentiating yourself from any competitor. You are already embracing the prospect as if they are a customer and creating even more value for them.

You are implementing the Conversion Equation as the basis of your customized report. The report shows that you understand the prospect's situation and have the help they need and want. The report can even be a simple one sheet. Nothing complicated. I remind you to send this within 48 hours of the meeting. Send this out by email and let your prospect know to expect the report so it does not get caught in a spam filter. Be sure to check in and verify that they have received the report just in case.

Send this report regardless of whether or not they buy instantaneously.

This secret sauce can make all the difference to your conversions!

CHAPTER 11
MORE TRANSACTIONS FAST

You may be feeling overwhelmed at this point because you have absorbed so much information. I will help you release any feelings of confusion or overcome in these final chapters.

First, in this chapter, I will review the entire process to score more transactions fast! Also, I will remind you how to systemize your marketing so your business can run on autopilot, saving you time, money, and any frustration you may currently be feeling.

Breathe! I've got your back.

Okay, while you now have a grasp of the proven Conversion Equation strategies, all you need to do is integrate them into one overarching system. As you are learning this integration, keep in mind that marketing is an ongoing, continuous process. Of course, the first part of the marketing system is to generate qualified "A" prospects. Some of the ways you will do this that we have covered are by:

- following the Conversion Equation
- creating a solid Core Unique Positioning Statement®
- hiring a professional marketing consultant who understands exactly how to implement the Conversion Equation correctly, has a proven

track record of growing business, guarantees your success and return on investment

So far, this book has given you a buffet of ideas. Now it is time for you to systematize and automate your marketing as much as possible. I want to not only help you create a business that brings you great wealth and allows you to help more people with your products and services, I want you, like my client family members and I, to have more free time for living life.

As a mentor of mine told me over 40 years ago, "Slow and steady wins the race." I could not agree more. You will be successful at having more transactions if you automate and systematize so you can leverage your time.

Grab your calendar, and let's begin this process. I want you to add each idea you will implement from the Conversion Equation and put those ideas on a marketing calendar. Then I want you to commit to taking those marketing actions.

If you try to do everything, I have given you at once, you will feel overwhelmed. This is why I help my client family members implement only two to four tactics per quarter. Trying to do too much is often a reason for failure

Step by Step

You will begin your marketing actions by knowing preciously and exactly with which narrow niche you will be working. You will then find out that niches specific problems they want to solve and the result they want—not need. You will do this by asking at least 15-25 or more people in that niche this question, "If I can help you get one result, and only one result, what result would you want to get?"

Notice how I will modify the question to fit my niche, and you can do the same thing. I might ask business owners who I know on social media and my database, "If I can help you get one result in your business, and only one result, what result would you want to get?"

I asked this exact question once I narrowed down my marketing consulting niche to small business owners. The answers I got were primarily about generating more qualified prospects fast. Then, I created my CUPS based on the result words my niche told me they wanted.

So, once you get enough answers to this question, you, like me, will have the right understanding of your niche, and you will not be guessing at what you think prospects want as a result of investing in your products or services. You will now create your CUPS following the formula I shared with you in the previous chapter:

"I help (who specifically with what problem) get (what result they told you they wanted) with (what proprietary system, method, process, or product or service) guaranteed (does not have to be a financial guarantee)".

After you have followed both of these steps, you will craft a way to interrupt, engage, educate, and offer in that order. I want you to immediately implement the Conversion Equation, which needs to become a routine part of your business. This entire process is proven to work and will bring you qualified prospects through reverse marketing.

Once you have qualified "A" prospects, you want to convert them into paying customers. You will need to decide on your pricing, products, and services you offer to your prospects. This means you must look at bundling and upselling, cross-selling and down-selling as well.

Then, you will be prepared with closing transactions using my secret sauce. Next, systematize getting testimonials from your customers. I suggest you create a system for asking for referrals (See Chapter 3) and immediately begin this process.

Also, decide what gifts you will give affiliates, endorsers, customers, and those they refer to you. Once you know what gifts or rewards you will be offering, it is time to find customers who will be endorsement partners and connect with other businesses who are potential joint venture partners. You will also begin your recall and reactivation system. This process will bring you qualified prospects who close themselves like clockwork. Asking for testimonials regularly and finding endorsement partners must become a natural system in your business.

I told you early on in the *Conversion Equation* the goal in my business—and for you and for my client family members—is to keep customers for life, so you that hunting for customers and qualified prospects becomes unnecessary.

Your customers will remain with your business as long as they feel you deeply care about them and they are not transactions. I remind you that Heart-repreneur® stands for integrity, transparency, and authenticity. I have had many client family members remain with me for more than 20 years! My client family members are also building these loyal relationships with their customers.

The goal is not to hunt for more qualified "A" prospects. Your business depends on satisfied customers who stay with you and refer others to you. My client family members are like my extended family, so I am always thinking of improving and making my services even better for them. I want to give them more and more value. I spend time working on my business each week to improve my systems and provide my client family members "WOW" service.

At Heartrepreneur LLC, we do not do "transactions" in the way most people define that word. We invite someone to purchase our products and services only if we know our consulting methods can help a prospect, and we are willing to embrace them, nurture them, and take them under our wings.

The Follow-up Program

Your final system for you to create is your follow-up program, an automated process you develop to keep in touch with all prospects that did not convert to paying customers immediately. You will begin by creating your report to send after each meeting with a qualified "A" prospect. You will then work on putting together your valuable and educational email drip campaign. You want to turn 99% of those who are not ready to purchase into your customers when they are ready to solve their problems. You will do this by staying in close touch through your drip campaign. Be certain you are using your drip campaign with your current customers, too, so that your business remains top of mind, and you continue to bring them value and demonstrate how much you do care about your customers.

Now is the perfect time to go back through the book, chapter by chapter, and create your systems. I want you to have more business, which means people do a transaction with you and pay for your products or services. Again, transactions are not seeking sales for the sake of sales, in my terms, they are helping the right people who have the exact problem your product or service solves to be able to pay your business for the results they want.

Transactions like these will happen if you apply what I have shared with you so far. I suggest you do not read the next chapters until you have put the pieces, I just reviewed here in motion in the step-by-step system as I have recommended. Create your CUPS, and devise a plan to interrupt, engage, educate, and offer.

Lay them out on your marketing calendar and get a professional marketing consultant for your small business to help you shorten this entire cycle and begin getting your conveyor belt of qualified prospects.

When you apply what you have learned in this book so far and create and follow these proven systems, your profits will soar. Sadly, I can also tell you that only about 3% of the people learning new information implement. I hope you will be an implementer who will be in my 3% club so I can celebrate you.

Once you have the Conversion Equation systems in place, you will continue to save time and energy and money as you keep using the same methods over and over. Keep doing what works.

I have been helping client family members put these systems in place for over three decades. I use them every day in my own business. Why? They are proven to work. I have used the exact systems I have shared with you so far to grow eight completely different multi-million-dollar companies of my own and to help over 6,000 business owners worldwide create more business success and greater wealth.

Do not reinvent anything that is working. You now have a proven system to bring your business more qualified prospects, close more sales, and make you more money. More transactions mean you are creating more incredible wealth in your business and making a real difference with your customers' products and services.

The Fundamental Marketing Systems

When you combine the three fundamental marketing systems in the Conversion Equation, you will have more transactions. Let's do a quick review of the three areas of focus.

Prospecting

Your prospecting system for attracting and generating leads consists of interrupting, engaging, educating, and offering—combined with your Core Unique Positioning Statement®. All of your marketing messages must speak to your specific niche, their problem, how your business and only your business, solve their problem. It also must include your guarantee or your low or zero-risk offer. This is your overall marketing strategy to acquire qualified prospects. Here are the tactics that are proven to work with this strategy:

- Irresistible offers with guarantees that are low and zero-risk
- Strategic endorsement partners
- Affiliates/joint venture partners
- Webinars
- Public speaking, events, seminars, workshops
- Drip campaigns
- Consumer Awareness Guides
- Information Guides
- SEO, pay-per-click ads and social media ads
- Articles, blogging, podcasting
- Books, e-books
- Trade shows
- Referral reward programs
- Networking

Qualifying and Converting

These are the strategies to put in place and systematize to qualify and convert your "A" prospects. We have discussed educational marketing with valuable content. This includes the follow-up report you send prospects after you meet with them, as well as your social proof (your influence), your drip campaign, sharing your Core Unique Positioning Statement® as well as your guarantee. This is exactly the strategy you will use to qualify and convert "A" prospects into buyers. Here are the tactics that are proven to work with this strategy:

- Sales conversion process with proven powerful questions and deep listening
- Special report
- Testimonials and case studies
- Drip campaign
- Video email

Boosting Perceived Value

Strategies you use to increase your products and services' perceived value include cross-selling, upselling, higher prices, bundling, WOWing customers, and referral and reward systems. These are the tactics that are proven to work with this strategy:

- Seminars, webinars, workshops
- Referral rewards
- Blogging, podcasting
- Drip campaigns
- Video emails

The easiest place to start generating revenue is to boost your current customer revenue first and reactivate past customers and recall current customers to purchase more frequently. Next, you will work on acquiring more qualified "A" prospects. And finally, you will have a system for closing them and following up with 99% of not now buyers.

All three of these areas are necessary for your success and must be continually expanded, enhanced, and improved.

CHAPTER 12
MORE PROFIT RIGHT NOW

I have mentioned that at Heartrpreneur LLC we offer a Profit Acceleration Session guaranteed to find a minimum of $10,000 in hidden marketing assets to any small business that is a startup. We guarantee to find at least $100,000 in hidden marketing assets for an established business, or we cheerfully refund the minimal investment a prospect has made to receive this personal consulting session. How can we do that? We can do this because we know where the hidden profits lie in every business and are experts at uncovering and revealing this.

While we are almost giving these sessions away, and our consultants are spending a lot of time with each prospect, we create high value and send the prospect a customized Blueprint of the actions they need to implement in their business. They can experience our value right away.

Before we began offering our time, our consulting, our Profit Acceleration, and our Blueprint, we looked at how we could create massive value quickly. We calculated the lifetime value of our customers. In my experience, almost every small business overlooks the powerful and tremendous leverage available to them just by concentrating on increasing their conversion rate through a variety of simple means. They also do not understand the lifetime value of every customer.

Lifetime value is a number you must know. This statistic is so important, and the effort you put in to improve it is vital. Your business can realize enormous profitability quickly by following my consulting guidance in this chapter.

⑤ CASE STUDY—SPEAKER TRAINER ⑤

Geri is a speaker trainer who hired me to make more money. She offers online courses and wants speakers to subscribe to her monthly speaker training program. What she was not aware of was how many inquiries per week were coming in from her website and through her social media channels, which were her primary marketing activities. She was spending a lot of money each month with on-line and off-line marketing and was not tracking the results of her marketing. I helped her create a simple system of tracking opt-ins and keeping names, addresses, emails, and phone numbers in a CRM. This way, she knew how each prospect found her.

Next, I guided her to start a drip campaign, which consisted of her Consumer Awareness Guide and Information Guide. She also worked with me to create an educational webinar, and prospects began to opt-in to watch this valuable training.

Then, I asked her if she could afford to hire a person who could make a five-minute call to each prospect who opted in and simply offered them a short phone call with her if they were qualified as an "A" prospect. At first, she told me, "no." Then I pointed out that we were cutting costs and no longer wasting money on marketing tactics that brought no results, so this was not an added expense. I also said if we figured out the lifetime value of a customer, she might see this differently. I helped her calculate the math of the life-time value of a customer.

Initially, she told me her average customer was valued at $997. Then, I asked her to go through an example of a purchase with me. She was shocked as we discovered that when an average customer purchased one of her on-line courses, and they invested $997 for that course, many of them also invested in her group coaching program for additional help. That program was $6,000. And some of her customers also added individual coaching for an additional

$5,000. Taking this further, many of her customers took a second course for another $997. If we add this up, her lifetime customer value is $12,994. She was off by $11,997!

I then asked her if her customers referred other customers to her. On average, she said each customer referred two people throughout their lifetimes doing business with her. Each of those customer's lifetime values would potentially be the same $12,994. Not to mention if they each referred another customer. Consider the lifetime value of those referrals!

Can you see that you must know this number and why it is essential for your business's health and wealth?

Once she realized the actual value of a customer's lifetime, she then agreed to hire a person to do these five-minute calls. We optimized the assets she had in place—her website, social media posts, and her educational webinar. We stopped the advertising money from going out so there was a decrease in her expenses even though she hired the person to schedule calls for her. Within less than 30 days she had 19 qualified "A" prospects to speak with and she closed nine of them into her $997 course.

Regardless of the business you own—wholesale, retail, service, or product-oriented—your business must have some type of ongoing effort to generate revenue. If you pay close attention to your conversion rate, your business will realize significant revenue and profit.

⑧ CASE STUDY—VIRTUAL ASSISTANT COMPANY ⑤

Marc is another client family member, and he owns a virtual assistant company. When he hired me, most all of his new business was generated by social media ads. He was convinced that some prospects who responded to ads were not converting because his company did not have a sales conversion process. Additionally, he did not know how to implement one that would work in his business.

I helped him find a person who would get on the phone and have a short conversation with prospects and minimal cost. With the simple addition of a trained salesperson, those website leads received follow-up calls, appointments made, and 35% of the people converted to become virtual assisting clients. This process alone increased his firm's sales from about $300,000 to over $450,000 in less than seven months.

Paying attention to your conversion rate is necessary. Unless you know not only the lifetime value of a customer and you track your conversion rate, you will not know if you have money to invest in marketing strategies or what tactics you might need to tweak. You might need to:

- improve your drip campaign,
- create a new message for your social media campaigns,
- change the message on your website, or in your autoresponders, or
- create a new offer or develop a new way of connecting with and contacting "A" prospects.

You must always track your conversion rate and the lifetime value of your customers. Measure everything. This is how to know what is working and to improve your profits consistently.

⑤ CASE STUDY—TAX PREPARER ⑤

Rob is a client family member who specializes in tax preparation. He had been sending out a drip campaign by email for years when he came to me for help. Rob wanted to increase his profits fast. After we created his Core Unique Positioning Statement® and started applying the Conversion Equation to his marketing, I made a minor tweak in the drip campaign he had been sending out for the past few years. The response to this new drip campaign doubled! His response rate doubled, and his profitability increased—and he had no additional marketing costs.

Rob was also hosting his business webinars and charging people $297 to attend his webinar training. I had him re-contact all of his webinar purchasers in his CRM. Going forward, we created a system to contact his future webinar purchasers automatically. Thirty days after their initial purchase of the webinar ticket, he sent out an automated email asking the webinar participant if they got value from the webinar and if they are using what he taught. He also asked a few other questions to find potential tax problems they might have. He then recommended additional products or services if appropriate.

By following this simple process, he generated $19,797 in additional revenue in only one month. The webinar purchasers had seen the value he provided, and they recognized his expertise. They also realized they had a need for more tax help, and he was the expert to turn to.

Add Cash Fast

Often a business comes to me for marketing consulting help because they feel desperate to bring money to their business fast. I begin by reviewing the client family members products and services, and then I put together a bundle of their products and services. They offer that bundle to prospects. Let me share an example of how bundling works to add cash flow to a business.

Let's say you own a spa. Customers come to the spa to get manicures for a charge of $50.00. Instead of offering the $50 manicure, you have been providing your customers, you now offer them a package of 6 manicures for the price of 5. The special package deal is available as an immediate add-on sale when they are checking out.

You can also offer your customers a bundle with six pedicures for the price of five, too, and let them know about this deal while at the check-out counter. As long as the add-ons have legitimate value, with definite appeal and high perceived value, your prospects will say "yes," and your $50 sale can soon become $250 per customer. Do that 10x a day, and you go from $500 income to $2,500 of income in one day.

Never forget that it is essential for your business success that you have happy, satisfied customers. This is why the initial transaction with your prospect is so important and why having a well-crafted and defined Core Unique Positioning Statement® and implementing well-run follow-up campaigns and customer service programs are so important. When you maintain a high degree of integrity, authenticity, transparency, honesty, and trust on the first transaction, you will be creating long-term relationships with your customers.

If you want more cash in your business, be certain when you do the first transaction with a customer, you have a way to "lock" your customer into a commitment to come back to your business over the next period of time

⑤ CASE STUDY—WINDOW WASHING COMPANY ⑤

Let's see how this strategy works again. My client family member, Vinny, owns a window washing company. I had him offer every customer a complimentary, home cleaning mirror kit valued at $50 if they purchase a window cleaning package of four cleanings per year. When he hired me for marketing consulting, he was typically washing a homeowner's windows only once per year. I wanted him to provide greater value and service to his customers, get paid more per transaction, and keep his customers long-term.

I crafted a strategy and helped him implement in his business created a higher than an average sale. His customers entered into a commitment to do business 4 times over the year instead of the window cleaning occurring just 1 time.

This strategy is one of the most neglected, yet predictably, effective techniques you can use to instantly improve the average value of every sales transaction and add more cash to your business. I want you to think of what additional products or services might fit or go along with your customer's initial purchase. You can offer these additional products or services at the time of the initial sale, later that week, or even 30-45 days later. This technique can be done by your website (think Amazon!) as well. Experiment with different packages, pricing, and other bundling combinations to see what works best in your business.

Keep building stronger relationships with your customers, while they enjoy more of your products and services—and get the results they are seeking.

Host an On-line or In-Person Event

Now that you know how to calculate the lifetime value of your customers and that you want to keep them for life, this next strategy will also help you get more income fast.

I suggest no matter what industry you are in that you plan a virtual or in-person event. During the event, you simply educate your current customers your area of expertise and have an interest. Instead of asking your customers to purchase a ticket to the event, provide them with a free ticket. Also, give them two additional free tickets to the event so that they bring two guests with them who would be interested in learning the information you will be presenting. You do not need to be a great speaker as you are only sharing your expertise and not your speaking talent, and you will not be closing or pitching at this event.

From my own personal experience and from the experience of my client family members, I know if 10 people attend an event like this, who are guests of current customers, on average two will become customers as a direct result of attending the event.

Recently, a client family member followed my advice 19 days after hiring me. She had 10 of her former customers attend the event, and she had 5 new prospects attend as well. All five of these prospects became patients of her naturopathy practice! Boom! Instant cash. And she did this event over Zoom so she had zero costs and put the cash right in her pocket.

I suggest that you have a few of your current or past customers "rave" about you by telling about their honest results and experience of being a delighted customer. Instead of you telling how great you are and promoting yourself, ask one of your satisfied customers or raving fans to introduce you and to say a few words about you and their actual results with your products and services.

Also, point out some of your customers successes with your products or services. You can also celebrate your customers and acknowledge them. Your customers will feel valued. They will know you care, and they are not simply a transaction when you take this approach. Their guests who are in attendance at the event will live vicariously through the results of others who are just like them. This will make your events even more effective. Having real customers of yours share their experience with your products and services with prospects who are just like them, will be setting up your credibility. This approach leads to more sales and at the same time reinforces and re-sells your own customers on your products and services as they hear themselves speak.

Two days after the event, I encourage you to send each prospect a short informational report summarizing the key points you shared during the event. I also suggest that you phone each prospect who attended to inquire what they got out of the event and to see if there have any questions that you can answer for them. If you want more fast cash, personally make these short calls. Why? In my experience, you will close 80% of these prospects when you make these calls yourself. If you delegate these calls less than 12% will end up purchasing your products or services. That is a huge difference and not worth the risk in my opinion.

Every time I use this tactic and a client family member of mine does, we expand our network and potential buyers and our incomes. This tactic is part of the education component of the Conversion Equation. And is easy to implement because your past and current customers are filling each virtual or live event for you! Just be sure you treat each prospect like royalty. Once again, these events are great ways to quickly get more customers while you grow your credibility.

My goal is to make you more money through fast generation of qualified "A" prospects and to do this at little to no cost to you. When implemented correct the Conversion Equation will bring your business amazing business growth results in a very short time frame.

CHAPTER 13

LIVING PROOF

The only thing standing in your way now is implementing what you have learned in this book and doing so in a timely and efficient manner. Heartrepreneur LLC is here to help YOU, and we invite you to schedule (www. tlwebinar.com/blueprint) your customized Profit Acceleration and Blueprint Session with us right now.

The content I have shared, when applied correctly, will bring you more qualified prospects, help you close more sales without selling, and grow your bottom line while giving you more freedom and free time.

In a moment, I will reveal several more case studies, demonstrating how other small businesses applied the Conversion Equation successfully. But first, I want to address some factors that will let you experience the results that other small business owners just like you are getting with my help.

Are You Ready to Take Action?

I have shared with you a proven formula, the Conversion Equation, that will quickly bring your business more prospects, more customers, and more income. Most business owners fail with their marketing because they do not have access to the information you now have. They lack marketing knowledge; they do not apply the Conversion Equation and are not using a proven marketing system.

They are too busy or too lazy to learn this marketing information and apply it in their business; they think they can do this without a marketing professional who fully understands the Conversion Equation and knows how to use it in their business. They have been sold a bill of goods by so-called marketing "gurus" who have them wasting time, money, and energy on things that are not fully proven to work to grow their business.

Great marketing is based on the skillful application of the Conversion Equation. There are essential skills that every great marketer, versed in the Conversion Equation, will help formulate, customize and apply to your business. The necessary skills are:

- Building relationships
- Effective communication
- Ability to correctly create a Core Unique Positioning Statement®
- Ability to write powerful, persuasive sales copy
- Willingness to find out what prospects want and need by marketing research
- Ability to implement and take fast action
- Having a laser focus on applying one concept at a time
- Effective use of time
- Being resourceful
- Perseverance
- Innovation
- Creativity

Triple Your Results

Many of my client family members have tripled their marketing results when they have gained great clarity about their target markets.

Pause and reflect: Who are you trying to sell your products and services to? Is this clearly defined in your marketing and advertising messages?

Your "message" in marketing is the promise you are making to your prospects. You must not only have the right message you need to know the right "media" to use to reach your target audience. The media is how you deliver your message

(direct mail, social media, pay-per-click, events, special reports, Consumer Awareness guide, Core Unique Positioning Statement°, videos, webinars, drip campaigns, website, blog, podcast, ads, etc.)

When you know your specific target market, have a clear marketing message aimed to solve their problem, and you select the perfect media to reach them, you can triple your expected results—just like my client family members have.

You and your business are not different from my client family members, and you can get the same kinds of results that the case studies have achieved. The Conversion Equation will work for your business, too. If you are ready to be the next success story, you will put what you have learned in this book into place right now.

I want to remind you that if you have the wrong media or wrong messaging or the wrong market, the Conversion Equation will not work for you. So, before you start marketing, always begin by identifying who is the exact niche for your products and services. Then, you must craft the perfect the right Core Unique Positioning Statement®, and next you will apply the Conversion Equation, and finally, you will select the right media for your business.

Your Market

You have to be certain that you have selected the ideal niche market that already wants what you sell and that they have identified a need for your products or services. You have to stand in their shoes, minds, and hearts and understand their high level of pain, frustration, or fear and how your product or service solves this. You must be the only business that can solve their pain, and must you must also be willing to guarantee their results. Of course, your target market must have not only the ability to invest in your products or services, but they must also have the readiness to do so. There must be enough people in that market to validate pursuing this specific niche. I suggest a least 10% of the market as a minimum.

Before you start marketing, be sure you have taken the time to get a clear picture of exactly who your ideal customer is. Not everyone will need or want your products and services. This is why you must take the time to get clear on this. You must figure out which prospects are most likely to invest in the products and services your business sells and then create your Core Unique Positioning Statement® so that you do not appeal to everyone. You only want to appeal to "A" prospects. Your best customer maybe someone who is already buying what you sell, but they are currently buying a similar product or service from another business.

I highly suggest you spend time researching and speaking with your ideal target audience to understand them fully. Listen not only to the words they use to describe their problems also pay attention to their feelings, their wants, and their needs. Read what they read. Watch what they watch. Listen to what they listen to. Go to seminars and events, both on-line and off-line, that they attend. Research who else is selling to them and how they are selling it.

Questions to Ponder

If you want to achieve the same success as my client family members have in the case studies in this chapter, then you must be able to answer these questions:

- Who is most likely to buy your products and services? Describe that person in great detail.
- What is their situation right now? What products and services are they currently using, and who are they buying from?
- What are the emotions and feelings that your ideal qualified prospects are feeling?
- How do they describe in their own specific words what their problem is and the results they want?
- What does a qualified prospect need to know that they might not be aware of when considering investing in your products and services?
- What are the key frustrations, problems, and distresses your qualified prospects have with other businesses providing similar products or services that you provide? What is their current situation if they use your type of products or services at present?
- What is most important to your "A" prospects when investing in what you sell? And specifically, why is that important to them?

- What are the top reasons your customers buy from you? Do not guess. Interview at least five current or past customers and learn this information directly.
- What solid proof can you provide that explicitly shows how your businesses and only your business uniquely delivers the benefits your customers want most, and how are you totally different from your competitors?
- What are your "A" prospects' beliefs and prejudices about the products and services you offer?
- Do ideal prospects already buy, or do they already understand what you offer, or do they need to be educated? If they need to be educated, remember, this is a critical step. Your marketing must focus on results, justify the investment to get the results your prospects want, and clearly communicate their pain with emotions and "hot buttons."
- Who else is selling products or services to your prospects, and how are they selling those?
- What trends are going on in the industry your prospects are in and in their personal lives?
- Do your prospects use jargon? How would they describe what your business does and the services or products your business provides?
- What are your prospects upset, frustrated, or irritated about—and who are they annoyed with?
- What is their greatest fear?
- What is the fastest and easiest way for you to gain access to qualified "A" prospects?

Rules, Values, and Beliefs

When I first started in the business consulting and coaching industry, I learned a valuable lesson. Instead of trying to influence prospects to invest in my products or services and persuade them to take action, I needed to understand that people's decisions are based on their values, rules, and beliefs. Let me define these ideas so you can earn from my mistake of not understanding these crucial concepts.

"Values" are the emotional states that are most important to a person. Perhaps you value freedom, integrity, or financial security. Whatever a person values, their actions, and decisions are aligned with their values. A "rule "is how a person gauges whether or not they are acting or behaving based on their specific values. A "belief" is a feeling of assuredness about something or someone. The beliefs someone holds run their actions, patterns, choices, and results in all areas of their lives. Some beliefs enable a person to achieve great results, while others' beliefs may hinder them from taking action and attaining what they truly desire. Rules and beliefs are related.

Let's see how values, rules, and beliefs apply to your marketing.

Example

If you believe that my ideas will not work for your business or believe that the Conversion Equation will not help your business make more money, underneath this belief are your rules. You are operating with this belief, and so you are holding a rule in place, often unconsciously. If I want to help you create a more successful business truly, I must understand your values. If I want to help you and have you invest in my small business marketing consulting, I need to find out, by asking you, what is most important to you. This question will uncover your values. Once I fully understand your values, I can uncover your rules and beliefs by asking why this is important to you. Finally, I can ask you questions about how you know when you believe and trust in a small business marketing consultant. Or, better said: How can you assure that you are not getting ripped off by a small business and marketing consultant?

As I deeply tune into your words, I discover your values, rules, and beliefs. Then I must share my Core Unique Positioning Statement® with you, proving that I provide what no competitor does. I give you my revolutionary guarantee because I know 100% that my Conversion Equation small business marketing consulting works—and I stand behind it. I will share my guarantee with you a 200% return on investment when you hire me. If I fail to achieve that, I give you all your money back, and write you a check for $5,000 for wasting your time. I know my guarantee and my Core Unique Positioning Statement®

stands alone in the market and will take away the concerns that you may have. You will find a benefit that is calculatable to you. I also make it clear that no one else in my industry makes the same claim and is willing to back up your investment.

I also give you proof that I am the best solution by sharing case studies and evidence right from the mouths of my client family members.

Can you see how I am working with my prospect's values, rules, and beliefs—and how I apply them in my marketing?

When I first began my business consulting company, I did not take the time or know that I needed to understand a prospect's values, rules, and beliefs. I did not fully understand my prospects; therefore, I often made incorrect assumptions about what messaging and even what products and services would appeal to them. This was a costly mistake that I am sparing you from.

Now we are ready to dive into some case studies. See which examples you can relate to and then apply in your business. Live vicariously through my client family members' success stories.

⑤ CASE STUDY-FINANCIAL ADVISOR ⑤

When Miguel first came to me for consulting help, he was not looking or sounding different than other financial advisors. His firm was missing a Core Unique Positioning Statement®. I helped him create a statement with no jargon or complicated words that would sound conversational. Here is what he initially told me about his business:" I help people make more money from the money they earn so they can potentially retire faster." I was not impressed, nor was I surprised he was getting few qualified "A" prospects each week. I helped him clarify what his audience wanted and how his firm provided their services different from all competitors and added in a guarantee.

His Core Unique Positioning Statement® is: "I help married couples who are thinking about their retirement create the financial ability to retire within five years, guaranteed potentially."

Notice a few things. First, he is not offering help for everyone. His target audience is married couples. And not just married couples, more specifically, those married couples who are planning their retirement. What does his audience want? To potentially retire in five years.

How can he make such a claim? He only works with "A" prospects who have the income to retire, and he is using the word "potentially" which means he is saying this "might happen" if certain conditions and requirements are met. His Core Unique Positioning Statement® does the work of reverse marketing, bringing him qualified "A" prospects regularly.

Once we nailed down his CUPS, we crafted a drip campaign. I helped him write articles, emails, and reports as if he were speaking just to one person instead of to all the prospects in his database. I had him also collect video testimonials of past clients sharing their own stories of how they were able to retire with his help.

He offered the Consumer Awareness Guide we created on his website and on his social media pages, titled, *The 10 DEADLY Mistakes People Make When They Hire A Financial Advisor: The Secrets to Having the Income to Retire!* His target audience had a high interest in this information, and the guide was downloaded regularly.

We created a special gift for his database and his social media following. This gift was to have a free Retirement Planning Session with his firm valued at $250. It was made clear that this was not a sales session and that his firm would generate a report of their recommendations with no strings attached as a service. His qualified "A" prospects saw the value in receiving the consult and report. Within two weeks of offering these sessions, he had 19 prospects schedule consults with his firm.

He had removed any risk for his prospects to schedule their sessions by letting them know up-front that he would cheerfully refund their money if they were not pleased with the session. He also was honest and transparent in his promotion of this consulting, explaining he was doing this to see if he could help the couple meet their retirement goals. And, he made it simple and easy for them to schedule the consult. They did not have to speak with anyone to get this scheduled, since he set up an automatic scheduler, such as Calendly. Because of this, they didn't have to worry about a sales pitch. He also had one clear, specific offer and action for them to take.

What can you apply to your business from this case study?

Case Studies-Sample Client Family Member Consumer Awareness Guide Titles

Having helped over 6,000 client family members to create effective titles for their Consumer Awareness Guides, I will give you a head start and an advantage of picking titles that work for your guide. I am sharing some of the most downloaded titles I have created. Do not use these exact titles. Modify them with your own words and use them as templates for creating your own Consumer Awareness Guide.

- Business Owners Beware: 71% of Business Owners Will Be Out of Business in a Few Months ... Unless You Know the 3 Simple Actions You Must Take NOW, You Could Be Out of Business
- Warning to All Business Owners: Your Website Could Be the Reason Your Business Isn't Getting New Leads!
- The Big, Hairy Secret That Most Social Media Consultants Don't Want You to Know About
- 6 Ways Most Financial Advisors Will Nail You with Hidden Fees, Unnecessary Costs, and Expensive Extras You Do Not Need
- Three "Shortcuts" Taken by Most Accountants That End Up Costing You Big Over the Long-Term
- Do You Really Want A Business Coach Who Makes YOU Do the Implementing or Do You Want a Done for You, Proven, Zero-Cost Consultant to Do It for You?
- Don't Even Think About Choosing a Real Estate Agent Until You Read This!
- FREE Report Reveals the Most Commonly Made, Costly Mistakes People Make When Hiring a Business Coach, and How to Avoid Them
- Case Studies-Sample Client Family Member Information and Idea Guide Titles
- I have created many titles for my client family members Information and Ideas Guides and am giving you some of the most powerful titles for creating your guides. Once again, do not use these exact titles. Modify

them with your own words and use them as templates for creating your own guides.

- How to Grow Your Retirement Income 25%-100%-The Secrets That You Don't Know
- How to Be Absolutely Certain Your Gym Revenues Grow by 25-100% or More
- How to Stop Wasting Money on Marketing That Doesn't Work
- Is Eliminating 100% of the Hassles, Headaches, and Worries About Getting New Customers and Keeping Old Ones Worth $16.00 a Day to You? Read This Now!
- 5 Months Ago, I Thought I Was Going to Have to Close My Business… Now My Business Is Valued at Hundreds of Thousands
- The Simple Marketing Strategy This Chiropractor Used to Increase Revenues by 29% Without Spending a Dime More on Marketing— Discover What He Did
- More Business Wealth the Easy Way
- How to Make Sure Your Children Get Enough Vitamins: Four Delicious Ways
- What Doctors Do to Keep Healthy That You Do Not Know
- Seven Types of Investors. Which Type Are You?
- 50 Ways to A Man's Heart: A Fascinating Guide for At-Home Cooks
- Receive $2,000.00 after Reading This
- Discover the Hidden Profits Lying Beneath Your Home
- New Shampoo Makes Your Hair Lighter and Easier to Manage!! Discover the Secret to Beautiful Hair
- 10 Secret Ways to Get Rid of a Cold
- Fifty Reasons Why You Should Read This Report That Potentially May Save Your Marriage
- An Amazing 2-Month Vacation You Get Paid to Take … For Women with Imagination Only
- Former Plumber Earns $89,000 in 3 Months as A Real Estate Agent
- Free Report: 10 Secrets to Better Lawn Care

- Announcing the Only Zero-Cost Consulting System Guaranteed to Increase Your Profits and Revenues 25% or More
- Business Growth System Eliminates Your Advertising Budget and Makes You Money!
- 10 Solid Reasons Why You'd Be A Fool to Go To Any Massage Therapist Who Does Not Do This
- Free Report Reveals 6 Critical Actions Every Small Business Owner Must Take to Prevent Their Business from Losing Customers
- Does Your Marketing Cost a Lot and Yield Poor Results? Discover an Easy and Zero-Cost Way to Eliminate All of Your Advertising Finally and Forever
- Hate Sales? Want Sales Professionals Do It for You at Zero Cost?
- 7 of the Biggest Sales and Marketing Headaches Plaguing Medical Day Spas, and How to Solve Them All
- I Used to Think Essentials Oils Had No Value. Now I Believe That They Are Actually Essential for Health
- I used to Have Horrible Adult Acne. Now I Enjoy Clear Skin
- How I Shed 25 Pounds in 6 Weeks Without Dieting or Exercising and Have Kept My Weight Off for Over 8 Years
- Pick one of these guide titles that you most resonate with and modify it for your business.
- Wait and see what happens!

⑤ CASE STUDIES—RISK REVERSALS & GUARANTEES ⑤

I always believe in guaranteeing everything you sell. I know this is key to having new customers purchase your products and services quickly. Risk reversal is the process of removing all the risk from the prospect saying "yes" to what you sell. The risk is not always about the money spent. These are some of the common fears and risks that my client family members have addressed through their guarantees:

- Financial loss
- Time wasted

- Inconvenience
- Feeling "had" or feeling stupid
- Intimidation (sales presentation, dealing with a salesperson)
- Appearing foolish to others
- Disappointment, frustration

Which of these will you use? Craft your guarantee based on the common fear or risk you have identified that your prospects most frequently have.

⑤ CASE STUDIES—DIRECT MAIL GRABBERS ⑤

I recommend using what I call "grabbers" or "lumpy mail" when doing direct mailings. The purpose of a grabber is to get the recipient to notice and read your snail mail piece. Here is a list of some of the grabbers I have suggested to my client family members that have worked well.

- Money and coins, fake money
- Aspirin, Alka-Seltzer
- Dice or poker chips
- Shamrock
- Worry doll
- Computer hammer (stress ball)
- Monkey
- Post-it notes, pens, note pads, erasers
- CDs/DVD's
- Raffle tickets
- Candy, gum
- Rubber skeletons, ghosts, eyeballs, (Halloween theme)
- Coffee mug
- Flashlight, magnifying glass
- The "envelope" itself (clear, plastic bag, Trick or Treat bag, mini trash can, www.sendaball.com , medicine bottle, mailing tube, etc.)

See which of these appeals to you. Here is a great source (www.orientaltrading.com) for additional ideas.

⑤ CASE STUDIES—GETTING EMAILS OPENED AND READ ⑤

When I help client family members craft their emails and drip campaigns, I want to make sure what they are sending out gets opened and is read. I give them two tips to send email on a Tuesday or Thursday, based on open rates we have documented through years of testing. The other is to personalize the subject line and the body copy. I help my client family members to create subject lines that interrupt, are irresistible, and invite curiosity. Feel free to model these email headings, which have made a big difference to my client family members' open rates.

- Are you coming Thursday, Bob?
- This e-mail may be the "butt chewing" you need…
- Don't take this personally, but…
- Mary, call me
- This will make your day
- Our office flooded today…see the photos

Notice in each of these case studies I have created subject headlines for the emails that are exciting. These same email headlines can be delivered in writing, verbally, by audio or by video. These headlines will excite a prospect enough to be curious and to engage with the rest of the message. These headlines instantly snap a prospect from downtime to uptime if the headline applies to their needs.

I recommend you not only experiment with different types of low and no-cost media to get your message to your ideal qualified prospects, but I also suggest that you test which headlines resonate with your "A" prospects. Once you discover an effective headline, keep using that headline until it quits working. Some never do! I have used the same headline for almost 26 years, and it continues to generate qualified prospects that result in huge of revenue. It is one of the ones listed above!

Just remember, with each of these case studies, the headlines I created for my client family members had one purpose—to interrupt their target audience.

⑤ CASE STUDIES—USING THE TELEPHONE ⑤

The most underutilized asset I see with my client family members is the telephone. Small businesses have gotten away from using the phone. Instead of hiding behind a computer or doing a mailing, posting endlessly on your social media accounts, starting a LinkedIn or a Facebook group, or hoping someone walks into your brick and mortar location, use the telephone. It is an effective, one-to-one marketing tool.

One of my client family members owns an auto repair shop. I had the shop put to use a recall and reactivation telephone strategy I helped them craft. They called prior customers and offered them a highly discounted emissions and inspection service. These customers were invited to bring in their automobiles for this service at a significantly reduced fee and get a free car wash. The results: 17% of those phoned did just that which lead to an increase in revenues and profits.

Another client family member or mine who owns a women's boutique identified 30% of their best buyers. We then assigned her three retail sale clerks a group of customers that they were personally responsible for calling. They began to call those customers regularly. When these clerks called, they invited these special customers and only them to a preferred sale for a limited time. The clerks made it clear this offer was only for VIP customers and not the general public. Again, recall and reactivation by phone is the strategy used here. The result? $156,000 in additional sales in one year.

Another client family member, an online course creator, hired a virtual assistant to phone all his prior customers who had ever purchased a course telling them a new course was coming out. As a prior valued customer, they could get the course during that week for 50% off before it was made available to the general public on their website. This resulted in a whopping 43% of purchases before the launch of their course.

The telephone provides a great way to recall and reactivate your customer base. If you have a customer base of any size, you have an asset worth a lot of money. When you have a customer who knows you, likes you, and trusts you—and has already purchased from your business and is pleased—they are most likely to invest in additional products or services on an on-going basis.

Keep in mind your lifetime value of a customer. If a customer purchases from you an average of 20 times over a lifetime, and each purchase is only $50.00 on average, that customer is potentially worth $1,000.00 in revenue to your business. To find the gross profit earned from this customer, you subtract out the cost of goods or services. Knowing this number is important because that is money that could potentially be spent up-front to generate one new customer for you—and you would break even.

The main advantage of this concept is that many businesses stop marketing in times of slowdown or a recession. This is the time to increase your marketing as your business will gain market share because you will win customers. After all, other companies have stopped communicating with their customers and prospective customers. You will spend no marketing money and gain more revenue and profits when you pick up the phone!

⑤ CASE STUDY—USING DIRECT RESPONSE ⑤ MARKETING WEIGHT LOSS PROGRAM

Most businesses also underutilize direct response marketing. Direct marketing is where your message causes the prospect to respond, raise their hand, and show interest directly. It is the foundation of reverse marketing. Prospects call your business, opt-in, message you, or email you because they are now responding to your offer. They are qualifying themselves. This means you save time and money hunting for "A" prospects.

Think about this: Wouldn't you prefer to have qualified prospects reach out to you daily?

I wrote this direct response marketing piece for a client who specializes in providing weight loss programs. Please do not use this word for word. Learn from this example and see how you might do something similar.

Your New Beginning Before the Holidays! Women Who Have Been Struggling to Lose Weight Can Lose 25 Pounds in the Next 6 Weeks—Guaranteed

And You Will Lose This Weight Safely and Without Feeling Hungry
Plus…You'll Feel Great and Increase Energy and Healthy Long Term!
Do You Know That Being Overweight Hurts More Than Just Your Looks?

According to the National Institute of Health, obesity is more than just a problem. It is, in fact, a disease with serious risks and consequences.

An overweight person is:

6 times more likely to develop gallbladder disease

5.6 times more likely to develop high blood pressure

5.4 times more likely to develop endometrial cancer

3.8 times more likely to develop diabetes

2.1 times more likely to develop an elevated cholesterol level

2 times more likely to develop osteoarthritis

Obesity can even exert its worst effect on your sense of self-esteem.

The National Institute of Health says, "Obesity creates an enormous psychological burden. In fact, in terms of suffering, this burden may even be the greatest adverse effect of obesity."

However, here's some good news!

The burden of being overweight isn't something you have to face alone!

For over 19 years, Traci Ross, M.D., has provided physician-supervised weight control and wellness programs for thousands of satisfied women just like you. Dr. Ross believes you are entitled to—and you *deserve* to—get professional help to shed the weight forever.

Her program's unique benefits called "Fast Fat Loss" is that it is different from every commercial weight loss program you have tried. Why? Dr. Ross treats your overweight condition as a disease, not just a problem. You'll receive a complete medical evaluation, including a nutritional assessment, medical history, laboratory testing, EKG, physical examination, and other tests when indicated.

This means your customized weight loss program will be safe and thorough. You'll become aware of any medical conditions you might have (high blood pressure, high cholesterol, diabetes, and arthritis). You'll feel better as these conditions improve or even clear up entirely as you lose weight on this program.

Under Dr. Ross's supervision, you will be guided through a six-week, personalized program with Dr. Ross's help every step of the way.

During your six weeks of "Fast Fat Loss" you'll enjoy:

- rapid weight loss (guaranteed 25 pounds gone in only 6 weeks)
- virtually no hunger
- safe weight loss under the Dr.'s medical supervision
- high energy levels
- preservation of lean body mass
- education and possible elimination of your symptoms due to being overweight

You will greatly reduce or even potentially eliminate depression, anxiety, irritability, exhaustion, dizziness, constant worry, cold sweats, fainting spells, headaches, indigestion indecisiveness, allergies, crying spells insomnia, nightmares, forgetfulness, high blood pressure, shortness of breath, and diabetes.

Get Started Now!

Go schedule your consult.

Get a free weight loss consultation with Dr. Ross at no charge.

Dr. Ross will help you during this consult, and you will be surprised you can finally lose the weight for much less than the cost of many commercial weight loss plans.

And, she'll help you keep it off with her consulting sessions, videos, and on-line community support so you can change your behavior permanently and keep the weight off for good.

Go to her website right now to get her free nutritional guide!

Go now to www.ABC.com.

Schedule your free no-obligation consultation before August 12th and get a bonus food calculator at no charge!

The results: She got 18 prospects in the first month and 4 new clients at $2597 each.

⑤ CASE STUDY—USING DIRECT RESPONSE MARKETING ⑤

Here is another sample of direct response marketing for a management training company. Once again, use your creativity and innovation to apply the same concepts to your business that I used when creating this direct mail piece.

Why Don't Your Employees Come to Work on Time?

Why don't they do their jobs? What happened to good old-fashioned honesty and work ethic?

Have you ever asked yourself these questions? In today's world, finding good employees is probably the single biggest challenge that leaders and managers face. Once you hire an employee why is motivating them, communicating with them, and getting them to do what needs to be done so tough?

Does Every Manager Have This Problem or Are You Alone?

Simply put, yes, every manager faces the same problem. They hire an employee and find they are not fully productive. Most businesses find they are performing at only a fraction of what they can because their employees just aren't giving 100%.

So, What Is the Answer?

The Answer is *You*.

Let me explain. Communicating with employees today is more difficult than ever. We have become a product of our environment. And our environment is filled with 10-second "sound bites," 30-minute television "resolutions" to crises (interspersed with 60-second messages on how to fulfill our every desire), traffic jams, e-mail, social media, and more. How do you communicate with people when their minds are filled with all this "stuff?" How do you motivate them? How do you get them to do their job?

Learn How to Break Through!

At RainMaker Communications Consulting Group, we know how to communicate with people. We know how to "breakthrough" and create self-motivated and productive employees—and we can teach you how.

You will learn how to communicate with employees, so they want to come to work on time.

We Will Show You How.

Come to our Transformational Leadership Communication Workshop on Friday, June 3rd at the Marriot Hotel at Plymouth Meeting and Germantown Pike. Coffee and a light breakfast will be served at 8 a.m. The training will begin promptly at 9 a.m. and conclude at 10:30 a.m.

We will have a panel discussion with some of the leading business owners and managers in the Blue Bell area about our incredibly successful techniques to improve your communication skills—get your employees to become self-motivated and more productive.

The cost is only $39.00 to attend but seating is extremely limited! Attendance is by reservation only-no walk-ins will be admitted!

Go to www.ABC.com to reserve your ticket now.

We limit seating to increase the effectiveness of what you will learn. This program will sellout.

Go to www.ABC.com right now.

Don't miss this one-time event!

Let us show you why your employees don't come to work on time and let's fix this problem now!

P.S. Our ability to improve your leadership communication skills can do wonders for your personal life as well!

CASE STUDIES—THE OFFER

When you communicate with prospects—and you have interrupted them and engaged them and educated them—it is then time to make them one clear offer. Simply saying, please call me doesn't work! Giving them too many actions won't work either. You want to make your prospects an offer that compels them to react. The offer must be low risk or zero-risk. You need to create an offer that is not only irresistible, but it must be stated clearly and concisely. Let qualified prospects know how valuable your offer is for them. Tell your prospects exactly how much they are saving or getting for free. Let them know how good your offer really is.

Here is an example of an offer I created for a client family member. Use this to spur on some creative and innovative ideas for your prospects.

The Offer

A free 1-hour marketing review and consultation. In this meeting, I will completely review your marketing efforts. I will uncover at least three things that you are not doing now, and that you can easily implement—that are no cost or zero-cost so you will rapidly grow your business. I will help you determine three critical numbers in your business that you probably don't know and, when we are done, I'll give you a marketing report card.

This review normally costs $1,295. I am giving away 20 of these absolutely free!

During your consultation I will do a market share analysis, competitor review, business profile report, close rate analysis, and much more.

In addition, you will receive a customized, step-by-step plan to grow your business by at least 30% in the next 8 months. My guarantee that we can make this work for your business. This written marketing plan and report alone is worth at least double the amount we charge.

The interview to gain the information is normally billed out at $1295 and the comprehensive plan to grow your business is absolutely priceless!

All of this for free if you act right now!

I even give you a complete guarantee if you are not totally ecstatic with the plan and report card, just tell me. I'll pay you $100 for wasting your time. You can't lose!!

You must tell your prospects why you are making a special offer. This "because" is essential. Here are some of the reasons I have crafted for my client family members. Again, feel free to model this and adapt these ideas to your business.

Why am I offering this to you? Actually, I've just helped one of my long-term clients with their marketing, and I am full of new and creative ideas to help my upcoming clients. I am eager to help others who are ready for business growth, and I am energized to do it quickly!

Why am I offering this to you? The answer is simple. A referral from you is worth thousands of dollars in marketing and advertising. It is business sense to make this offer to you.

Why am I offering this to you? I could give you some smoke and mirrors answer, but I always speak the truth. The truth is this offer is good business and makes sense. Why? Two out of three people who receive our Lifestyle Guide choose to do business with us at some time in the future. I save hours of time and save the cost of traditional advertising to find that many good clients. How about that for an honest answer!

Why am I offering this to you? We've just expanded our Pilates centers capabilities and would like to find more clients. See? An honest answer. We do a lot of unusual things at our Pilates center that I think you'll like.

⑤ CASE STUDIES—ACT NOW ⑤

You want your qualified prospects to act now. To get them to take you up on your offer I suggest you reward your prospects for doing what you want. Through creativity and innovation, you can create a bonus for taking fast action. Keep in mind the bonus must create value for your target audience. Here are some actual things I have created for my client family members to get their qualified prospect to act fast. Again, I invite you to model them and apply them in your business.

Call before September 5th, and I'll give you a video training series to get more qualified leads fast. These videos have my most powerful marketing ideas and normally sell for $197—and they are your free today!

Go to my website today. Download our free report, *15 Quick Ways to Make Your Home Sparkle—Naturally*. Opt-in for your free information-packed, 11-page report that is just crammed full of great organic home cleaning ideas. Yours free with no obligation today.

Have you heard about our amazing WOW Customer Service Webinar? It's an incredibly ingenious way to drive customers back into your business again and again and again. Register right now for the webinar. Do it before Tuesday the 11th, and I'll also send you the PowerPoint slides and note pages of this remarkable training absolutely free! You'll be amazed at the power that this will have to keep your customers coming back to do even more business with you.

⑤ CASE STUDIES—CALL TO ACTION OFFER ⑤

When you make your offer, using the Conversion Equation, you must have a call to action. There must be a reason to act now or they will not. When you state your call to action, you want to keep it short. I find that up to three sentences works well. Here, I share some of the calls to action I have created for client family members that get a great response. These are guides for you to follow.

I know this offer will have an overwhelming response, and I can only handle a few clients at a time. Wouldn't you love to be one of the lucky few? Act Fast!

We only have a few of these incredible books to give away, so call us right now.

Because of the very intensive attention I give to each of my patients, I can only handle a few at any one time. If you would like to be one of the lucky few schedule your appointment right away.

This offer is being jointly promoted with the Speech and Hearing Clinic, and it expires on February 5th! Opt-in right away to take advantage of this incredible opportunity!

We only have 50 slots for the webinar training available so hurry and be one of the first and save your spot!

A free website checklist and a website roadmap to getting to number one on Google is yours now. You must opt-in now to take advantage of this offer!! Go to www.XYZ.com

Call us before Friday the 7th to receive your Consumer Awareness Guide, *The 9 Deadly Mistakes You Are Making As An Author*, for free! This guide will be a huge game-changer in your writing career.

The incredible Profit Acceleration tool that finds you a minimum of $10,000 in your business is yours now. This is a no-obligation session valued at over $10,000. Schedule now using this link.

As you can probably tell, this is not a mass e-mailed letter. I chose to make this offer to you for some very specific reasons. Call me and I'll explain what those reasons are.

CHAPTER 14
ARE YOU NEXT?

As you can see, there are many skills you must be great at to increase your business and marketing success. These include:

- your relationship and communication skills,
- your ability to write powerful, persuasive sales copy,
- your willingness to spend a lot of time on research, your fast implementation,
- you being laser focused on correctly applying one step of the Conversion Equation at a time, then perfecting the entire formula through measuring and testing, managing how you spend your time,
- being resourceful, and,
- finally having perseverance.

You want to avoid the common mistakes most business owners make in their marketing which is not having the right marketing knowledge or using proven marketing systems. If you are not getting qualified prospects daily, you are not an expert in building relationships with prospects and are not properly positioned to have prospects resonate with your messaging. You may be using advertising like ads, blogs, and podcasts that get no results or marketing that gets no response.

Let's do a quick check-up of your current marketing.

Marketing Check-Up

- Look at your current prospecting and lead generation. Are you using these strategies?
- Core Unique Positioning Statement®
- Direct response marketing
- Message to market match
- Niching
- Integration of your Core Unique Positioning Statement®
- Multi-media marketing
- What about these tactics?
- Affiliates/joint venture partners
- Social media
- Website
- Landing pages
- Blogs
- Podcasts
- Articles
- Email
- Drip campaigns
- Irresistible offers
- Webinars
- In-person or virtual workshops and/or seminars
- Consumer Awareness Guides
- Information Guides
- Books, e-books
- Trade shows
- Networking
- Strategic endorsement partners
- Referral reward program

- Reactivation
- Recall

Be honest in your evaluation and assess where you are currently in your marketing efforts.

Now, let's look at your qualifying and converting abilities and how successful you are in this area at the present time. Which of these strategies do you have in place at the current time?

- Educational marketing
- Consumer Awareness Guide
- Information Guides
- Core Unique Positioning Statement®
- Testimonials, case studies
- Guarantee
- Low or zero-cost offers
- Drip campaigns

And what about these tactics? How many of these do you have in place that are effective at qualifying "A" prospects and converting them without selling?

- Sales/conversion process using powerful coaching questions
- Education Guide
- Information Guide
- Endorsements
- Written, audio, and video testimonials
- Case studies
- Drip campaign follow up
- Email broadcasts
- Consumer Awareness Guide

In the area of perceived client value which strategies are you using with great success?

- Continuity programs
- Cross-selling
- Bundling
- Upselling
- WOWing customers
- Strategic endorsement partners
- Affiliates/Joint venture partners
- Referral reward systems
- Increased prices due to increase value perception

And which tactics are you using that are bringing you the results you desire?

- Coaching/consulting/training, etc.
- Seminars (virtual and/or in-person)
- Webinars
- Workshops (virtual and/or in-person)
- Contests
- Referrals rewards
- Customer appreciation gifts and/or events
- Blogging
- Podcasting
- Article writing
- Drip campaigns

Which of the marketing fundamentals are currently in place to grow your business successfully and to create the wealth you desire from your business?

- Is your current marketing using these basic fundamentals?
- You have a clearly defined and very specific niche market.
- You understand your target market demographics, as well as the psychographic make-up of your market with data backed-up research—not by guessing.

- You have surveyed at least 15 people in your niche market and clearly can articulate what their key frustrations are, their buying reasons (what they want), how they make decisions, and what their current process is for buying the services/products you offer.
- You have researched your competitors and know their strengths and weaknesses.
- Based on the data you have collected from the research you did of your target market and competitors, you have constructed (or enhanced!) your Core Unique Positioning Statement® and your offering as well as your business operations and customer service systems to deliver what your customers want better than all your competitors and uniquely, too.
- You have clearly and confidently defined what your business does better than any of your competitors, and you have crafted a convincing argument as to why a prospect should choose you over the other options available to them.
- You can back up your marketing claims with customer testimonials (at least 10 or more) that outline the specific results you have delivered for customers.
- You have a contact relationship management system in place for capturing, tracking, and communicating with your prospects and customers—and you are continually adding new, qualified "A" prospects through a variety of marketing campaigns.
- You have branded your business and your branding is consistent in all communications, such as your email signature file, on your website, in your emails, with your Consumer Awareness Guide, and your Education Guide, and your opt-in pages, your webinar, your social media headers, your business cards, your brochures and flyers, your proposals, etc.
- Now, let's look at your advanced marketing systems. Which are in place and working well?
- You have great sales copy on-line and off-line that follows the Conversion Equation and makes it clear who your ideal customer is and what problems you solve for them. Your value proposition is expressed through

your Core Unique Positioning Statement® and explains why someone should buy which is backed up with actual proof of your claims.

- You have an irresistible offer that is low or zero-cost and that is on an opt-in page as well as the home page of your website. Prospects can provide their contact info you to use to follow up.

- You are automatically tracking unique visitors to your website, most popular search terms, and your on-line conversion rate and you are converting visitors to qualified leads regularly

- You have a powerful, compelling way to interrupt, engage, educate, and offer

- You have an effective Consumer Awareness Guide, Education Guide, Information Guide, and webinar that provides value to your prospects and educates them on what to look for when investing in your category of products or services.

- You have a referral marketing system in place to ask for, reward and follow up on referrals.

- You have a sales process for following up on new leads and closing them and your process facilitates at least a 75% closing rate.

- You have a system to qualify "A" prospects.

- You are comfortable and/or a member of your team is, in asking powerful questions, uncovering problems, and revealing frustrations and suggesting solutions.

- You have a process in place for clearly understanding prospect's buying criteria.

- You have a compelling reason for prospects to buy now.

- You have in place cross-sell and upsell campaigns that are proven effective and you use them with current customers at least once a quarter.

- You have at least one recall and one reactivation marketing system that you use for out at least monthly communication with current and former customers, both on-line and off-line.

- You have affiliate, joint venture, and strategic endorsement partner relationships—and are actively seeking new partners—and also taking full advantage of the relationships you have with current partners.

Next, review some enhanced marketing systems you will need to have in place to grow a six-, seven-, and potentially even an eight-figure business. See if you currently have any of these:

- You are implementing at least five proven ways to generate qualified "A" prospects every week.
- You have a monthly system to bring you referrals every single month.
- You have a systematized on-line and off-line media marketing message that brings you qualified "A" prospects.
- Your website is ranked using Search-Engine Optimization (SEO) tactics, and your website is in the top five in search engine result pages for your top 10 keywords.
- You have in place a monthly tracking system for your average customer transaction, number of qualified prospects, your conversion rate, your cost per lead, your cost per customer, you know the lifetime value of your customers, and you are tracking a return on investment for all of your marketing campaigns by measuring the leads and sales you are generating.
- You have 5 or more effective lead generation campaigns in use and have been using them for at least 12 months to establish your brand.
- You are using organic social media marketing that is resulting in quailed "A" prospects weekly.
- You have a minimum of three affiliate or joint venture partners who enthusiastically and regularly promote your products and services to their customers.

A Few Reminders

I want you to be ready to actually grow your business now. Let's spend a few minutes making sure you are taking away the key points in the *Conversion Equation.*

- Do you know the exact, specific, narrow and small niche you are targeting and offering your products and services to?

- Have you created a Core Unique Positioning Statement® with a clear promise for this particular market?
- Have you chosen the best ways to deliver your marketing messages—drip campaign, blogging, podcasting, webinars, website, ads, etc.?

Before you jump right in and start marketing you want to be 100% certain your ideal target market wants the kinds of products and services you offer and that they have expressed an identified need and more importantly a want for your products and services. This means you must take time to become aware of the pain, struggle, or frustration or fear your target audience has and find out their exact words to describe their situation. Don't guess. Ask your audience:

- "If I can give you one result and ONLY one result, what result would you want"?
- Survey 15-25 prospects and find out what is on their minds and hearts and stand in their shoes. And be certain your business solves that problem.
- Can you guarantee your results?
- Does your ideal target audience have the ability and are they ready to invest in your products or services?
- Are their enough members of this niche to validate enough potential purchasers?

Why do I want you to answer these questions before you jump into marketing? This is because unless you have a very clear picture of who your "A" prospect is, your marketing will cost you time, money, and energy for little to no return on investment. Remember, not everyone needs or wants what you sell.

ONE Market

Only focus on one market. A brand that is all over the place and looks scattered causes their prospects to become confused. As I often say to my client family members, "a confused mind doesn't buy." You don't want to sell everything to everyone. Be certain that you keep in mind your best customer is often someone who is already buying what you sell but buying it from someone else. Take time to interview or to conduct focus groups with your target audience so you can deeply listen to them and understand them. Listen to the language they use to describe their problems, their wants, and what they say about your products and services. Read what they read and watch what they watch. Attend meetings they go to and listen to them. Research who else is selling to them and how they are selling to them.

Credibility and Trust

I find many business owners get so excited with the information in the *Conversion Equation* that they go right into marketing actions and have not thought about how to build credibility and trust with their audience. If someone who is an ideal qualified "A" prospect reads your marketing campaign or hears your CUPS, there are only five reasons why they will not buy. Understanding these will help you do your marketing correctly building credibility and trust first.

People don't buy if:

- They do not believe you.
- They do not trust you,
- They do not see the value for the money invested.
- They do not see the need for what you have. They don't have any pain that causes them to desire a solution that your product or services solves, and there is no sense of urgency to remove that pain now.
- They do not afford your products or services.

You cannot affect their lack of money too much. You can provide payment terms or help them get funding, and that's it. You might be able to slightly impact building on their pain and creating a need. Where you can really improve your credibility and trust is by directly addressing their belief in you, their trust in you, and helping them to see the value you provide.

If you start marketing without first building credibility, you will not have great success. You can build your credibility, even if you are new in your business, by having strategic endorsement partners, testimonials with specific results, and even testimonials about who you are as a person. If you have been in business for a while, put together case studies with specific results. If you are a start-up or an established business, be sure to share your guarantees, too.

Another way to gain credibility is to quickly become an influencer in your industry. You can do this by writing a book, writing articles, blogging, podcasting, being a guest on radio, TV shows, and podcasts, hosting your own webinars, and appearing as a guest on other people's webinars, hosting your own summits or participating on summits, giving on-line and off-line workshops, through public speaking, etc.

Your influence will grow as you also share your Core Unique Positioning Statement® everywhere and are consistent with it.

Your testimonials will help convince prospects that you are a credible expert and your business is trustworthy. Keep in mind that prospects are asking themselves this question, "Why should I buy from you?" All endorsements and case studies act as testimonials that will help convince prospects and that will give them more trust when they hear or read the words or watch the videos from people just like them. If your testimonials also overcome common sales objections and verify claims, prospects will trust your business and buy products and services from your business faster, too. Just be certain that you have testimonials from peers in your ideal prospects' niche so they can relate to people just like them.

You can never have enough testimonials!

Stories

I have one more item for you to consider before you launch your *Conversion Equation* marketing. I want you to put together some unique stories based on your business and life experiences. Stories are one of the most powerful ways to grab and hold a prospects attention, and to make a point and also are used to sell an idea, and subsequently, to sell your products or services.

My very first business mentor was Zig Ziglar. His entire teaching approach as well as his sales approach was based on the use of stories. Why? This is because stories are recalled and related to. Think about it. Even the Bible is a series of stories.

Adults read fiction books more than non-fiction books with fiction outselling non-fiction by 100 to 1.

Begin thinking of some stories you might use. Stories can be used in various forms. You can tell a parable type story to teach a lesson. You can also talk about something you used to think or believe in business or life that you no longer believe. This type of story is based on being a skeptic at one time and how you have turned into a true believer and transformed your thinking and why you have. I depend heavily on customer stories and case studies in all of my marketing as well. You might also want to create your before and after story. This is where you would craft a story based on some problem you used to have, how you alleviated the problem, and what result you are enjoying as a result of getting rid of the problem.

And finally, for even more credibility, share the story of how you became the expert in your industry.

All stories, of course, must be factual, and you should be able to tell them with ease.

Before you start fully applying the Conversion Equation come up with at least one story to use when you engage your target audience.

Lead Generation Mistakes to Avoid

You are almost ready to begin your proven marketing system. I want to share a common mistake many business owners like you make and help you avoid this mistake right from the start. Do not assume because you are giving a no or zero-cost offer to your prospects that they will instantly desire what you are offering even if it is very compelling. You will still need to market your offer. People are busy. They are bombarded with marketing messages. Even those messages that are very relevant to them. However, people have limited time and to download a report, watch a webinar, call for a consultation, come to your place of business or take any action, that takes up some of their time. The price of a prospect's time is high. They typically place great value on their time.

You are asking someone to be inconvenienced and to take time out of their crazy-busy day to do something that might be a waste of their time. This is why you have to be certain your no or zero-cost offer does not sound like a sales pitch in disguise, and you must "sell" this even if it is free.

If a prospect even thinks they might be sold or are going to deal with a salesperson, the chances are they will avoid your no or zero-cost offer no matter how compelling your offer is and how much they desire your offer.

I call offers "lead generation magnets" because you offer something that will hopefully pull in interested prospects and sort, sift, and separate the "A" prospects from the masses. This is where reverse marketing magnetizes your "A" prospects to your business. Your no or zero-cost offer will not be acted upon by your target audience unless it draws them in. Your offer must be of high-perceived value to your prospects with little or no risk or downside for prospects to request it or to consume it.

It also must provide a real, concrete solution to a problem that the prospect wants to resolve. And it must deliver a result the prospect wants to achieve or both. Don't forget you still need to sell the offer as though it costs money, even if you are giving it away for free. People will still hesitate to take you up on your offer as it takes their time and fear being sold.

Of course, the offer has to be relevant to what products and services you are selling, and it has to facilitate the sale. For example, a free report on how to cook fast healthy meals every day would be a good offer or lead generation magnet for a program on healthy and quick eating. It might not be a good lead generation magnet for home food delivery meal-planned services.

The offer must sell the concept behind your products and services. I share my free training (www.tlwebinar.com) which teaches my philosophy and mentions the mistakes businesses are making—and gives the essence of my concepts as my primary lead magnet. Think of your lead magnet as a well-orchestrated plan to ultimately attract and convert prospects who are "A" prospects into paying customers.

You can use free offers or low cost as your lead magnets such as:

- Audits
- Seminars or workshops (on-line or off-line)
- Webinars

- Surveys
- Checklists
- Templates

Now it's time to make a plan and get into action.

CHAPTER 15
CREATE YOUR MARKETING PLAN

N ow it is time to create your marketing plan based upon what you have learned from the *Conversion Equation*. When you read a book and take no action from what you have learned, I refer to that as "shelf help." The book does not transform your business or your life and sits on your shelf, and no action is taken.

I wrote this book to provide real value and true help for those who apply this simple, proven marketing formula and want real change in their business and wealth.

Follow this marketing plan to ensure you get value from the breadth and depth of teaching and experience built into the Conversion Equation. I truly care about you and your success, so I urge you to:

- Set goals for your business and your marketing.
- Go through each chapter again and highlight key points.
- Pick two ideas or strategies to implement in the next 30 days.
- Review those ideas or strategies and schedule the details of implementing them.
- Put your plan into action.

- Measure your results and tweak what you are doing to improve your results before adding or changing your ideas or strategies.

I also suggest you write out your marketing and business goals in quantifiable terms. One of the best things you can do right now is also to brainstorm based on the ideas in this book. Keep a list of the ideas that you are most excited about to implement in the future. Just don't forget you must use the entire formula— *interrupt, engage, educate, and offer.*

I always tell my client family members to overestimate how many touches will be necessary to generate a response or hit their goals when they predict how many touches or how many marketing campaigns they need to use. This will depend on your goals, the effectiveness of your Core Unique Positioning Statement®, and your niched target market. Be certain all your marketing campaigns include not only a sale, but also a way to thank customers for purchasing, a system of asking them for referrals, testimonials, and a planned upsell. Systematize all your marketing as much as possible so you have more freedom and free time. When I find something that works, I simply rinse and repeat and automate like my free training webinar or lead generation videos.

Next Actions

Start with the lowest hanging fruit to bring your business money fast and to take advantage of the easiest ways to bring in that income. Here is your three-month action plan.

Month One

- Begin a referral and reward program for past and current customers.
- Upsell current customers with a program or product or service you have not offered them to give them better results and offer that to them right away.
- Create a drip campaign and follow-up system for all prospects you currently have and use it with them and all prospects.
- Look at your business, carefully analyze and improve your guarantees, powerful closing questions, and financing terms.

- Make a low-cost offering to all unconverted leads.
- Put everyone into a database or in a Contact Relationship Management system.
- Use the phone to build relationships and to reactivate and recall customers.

Month Two

- Create your Core Unique Positioning Statement® (CUPS)
- Use the CUPS in all your emails, social media, website, business cards, etc.
- Create an opt-in page for your free offer.
- Begin gathering testimonials and endorsements.
- Create your interrupt headline.
- Add your interrupt headline to your website, social media headers, email signature file, etc.
- Write at least three short blogs for your website.
- Send out weekly drip campaigns to touch your database and add value to their business and or their lives.

Month Three

- Refine your CUPS and be certain you are using it everywhere.
- Create and leverage affiliate partnerships and joint venture relationships as well as strategic endorsements.
- Send out a piece of lumpy direct mail.
- Attend online or off-line webinars, meetings, networking groups where your target audience hangs out.
- Create your Consumer Awareness Guide.
- Create your Education Guide.
- Re-read and review your notes from the *Conversion Equation*.

CHAPTER 16
INVEST IN PROFESSIONAL HELP NOW

I just gave you a three-month basic action plan; however, to effectively and successfully implement the proven Conversion Equation, I strongly suggest hiring a small business marketing consultant. This consultant will be your trusted advisor who will assure the strategies and tactics are not only implemented, they are correctly implemented and applied.

The right small business marketing consultant will help you:

- identify your specific niche, even if you think you have done that
- identify the one result your target audience is ready to buy
- craft your CUPS
- identify the perfect marketing mix
- apply the Conversion Equation to reach your "A" prospects \
- implement each marketing strategy identified in the *Conversion Equation* \
- identify your hidden marketing assets
- provide you with proven Guerrilla Marketing strategies
- set up systems for your business
- monitor your results, and
- tweak your campaigns

- This professional will ensure that you get the best results from your marketing efforts.

When to Hire a Marketing Consultant

How do you know when to hire a marketing consultant? When you,

- Are ready to implement the Conversion Equation—now?
- Need a proven system and the specialized marketing skills and expertise that you or your business lacks
- Want a professional, external viewpoint to your business, sales or marketing challenges
- Need a new perspective on lead generation, conversion, sales, customer retention and any of your current marketing strategies
- Are serious about business growth and are ready to increase your revenues and profits with proven no or low-cost marketing versus trial and error
- Are tired of creating content, spending money on ads and wasting your time, money and energy on marketing that brings you little to no financial results
- Want to focus your business on overall operations and product and service development instead of costly marketing mistakes

What Skills Should a Professional Marketing Consultant Have?

The right marketing consultant will be well-versed in the Conversion Equation, create a CUPS, and mix both technical and soft skills. The consultant will have a track record and be skilled in marketing, business, communications, and psychology. They will be able to provide consulting on the following marketing process:

- Conversion Equation implementation
- Creating the perfect niche
- Developing and implementing the right CUPS
- Online marketing
- Off-line marketing

- Drip campaigns
- Establishing endorsement partners
- Building joint venture and affiliate relationships
- Copywriting
- Advertising
- Guerrilla Marketing with no and low-cost proven strategies
- Public relations
- Direct response marketing
- Uncovering hidden marketing assets

Professional small business marketing consultants are not coaches. A coach does not give advice, strategies, or answers. They rely on you to find your own answers. Small business marketing consultants are advisors and strategists who use coaching tools to help you—if and when necessary; however, the big distinction is that a coach is not a consultant and they give no advice.

A consultant, however, can use coaching tools if needed but unlike a coach. They will give you their skills, knowledge, and expertise, provide you with proven answers, and help you implement instead of doing your own thing that might not work. A consultant has a very large toolbox, and coaching is a tiny tool in their arsenal.

Your small business marketing consultant should be creative yet practical, results-driven, and focused on consumer behavior and the psychological understanding of target audiences. This person must be willing to collaborate with your company to achieve the best possible results for your business that are aligned with your business's goals.

I recommend you engage a small business marketing consultant who displays flexibility, collaborative energy, and creative thinking. These skills are all essential to a successful relationship between the small business marketing consultant and your business.

Essential Factors for Selecting the Right Marketing Consultant

Hiring a small business marketing consultant might feel like a big step; yet, this is essential for your business's health and long-term success. I know that hiring someone to help with marketing for your business might not be a step you have considered taking and that there are a lot of factors you need to consider before selecting the right small business marketing consultant.

First, I suggest you look at the expertise the consultant will bring to your business. Marketing is constantly changing and requires flexible strategies. It is something you most likely are not an expert in. You want to hire a small business marketing consultant who has a track record of proven success and is willing to guarantee your success and offer you a no-risk way to get the results you want from your marketing.

The small business marketing consultant should be able to take on your specific marketing challenges and help you meet and exceed your goals. This may sound odd to say; however, before I tell you why you should hire a small business marketing consultant, first let me tell you the reasons why you shouldn't.

Do Not Hire a Small Business Marketing Consultant If...

You are expecting magic from them.

They will not be magicians who pull rabbits out of hats. Marketing takes effort. They will work to catapult your business results and cannot do this overnight. If anyone promises you overnight results, run fast. While marketing shortcuts may help you see results in the short term, they will always come back to bite you. A small business marketing consultant will not miraculously turn your business around in a few weeks—and if you think they will, do not hire one because you will be disappointed. The right small business marketing consultant will get to know you and your business and create a strong marketing strategy before applying tactics to your business. When they do apply tactics, they will use Guerrilla Marketing and Hidden Marketing Assets—proven tactics to achieve your business goals.

You are not willing to invest in your business.

Investing in the right small business marketing consultant will pay dividends for your business. As your business increases, if you are not willing to invest in addressing innovation and creativity with your business challenges, you should not hire a small business marketing consultant. You must be serious about being in business and building a successful, profitable, and sustainable business. With the new volume of qualified "A" prospects and the fulfillment of products and services for the new stream of customers generated, you must be willing to handle the business growth. If you do not want to grow and are not interested in having a long-term business, save your money, continue with your hobby or possibly consider getting a job.

You are not committed to marketing long-term.

Marketing is not a single event. Marketing is an ongoing process. It is a necessity for every successful business. Remember these words, "always be marketing." You do not do some marketing one time and hope that you will reap the benefits of that marketing for eternity. Be a realist when you think about marketing. If you are not willing to invest in your marketing long term, you are not committed to your business growth and hope your hobby eventually grows or you can consider getting a job.

Why You Should Hire a Small Business Marketing Consultant...

Your marketing is not working.

If your marketing is not bringing you a conveyor belt of qualified "A" prospects regularly, this is a sign that your marketing is not effective. This is almost always because you are not a marketing expert, and you lack proven marketing strategies. You may be listening to "fake experts." If you are frustrated with your marketing, you need a real, proven, guaranteed, and effective marketing strategy that, in my experience, only a true marketing professional can provide for you. Suppose you are not sure who your "A" prospects really are. In that case, you are not completely different from all potential competitors, and you do not fully understand the psychological reasons why customers buy from you, your marketing will fail to reach its potential. It will not be as effective as it can be.

Effective marketing is based on proven strategies and builds momentum with consistent application of proven tactics. The right small business marketing consultant will first spend time delving into your business and then will build your marketing strategy. Finally, they will help you implement the right tactics to execute that strategy. Strategy always comes before tactics. If you do not start "with the end in mind," as author and educator Stephen Covey said, you will simply be throwing some tactics out there and hoping and praying something might stick and get you some result.

You do not have the time to dedicate to your marketing.

Without dedicated time and energy for marketing, your business will not grow. Marketing requires constant focus, action, and the right implementation. Sustainable business growth will not come without consistent marketing. It is a fact! If you are feeling as if you do not have enough time for marketing your business, then you absolutely must hire a small business marketing consultant who will help you leverage and optimize your time "working on" and "not in" your business as author Michael Gerber stated. If you focus your brilliance on what you love and enjoy in your business, your business will give you more satisfaction. Having a small business marketing consultant help, you dial your marketing in will ensure your business is successful and give you more freedom and free time.

You lack marketing expertise or skills.

You may lack marketing skills and yet you may believe that you need to do everything in your business yourself. You might be trying to find customers, convert prospects, create products and services, pay bills, do human resources, handle budgets, read emails, engage in social media posting and commenting, write promotional copy, work on your website, and much more. You probably are not highly qualified to do all of these things. Instead of creating a business where you are trying to be an expert in sales, customer service, operations, and marketing functions, get professional help. You might be making some very costly mistakes that can seriously harm your business going forward. This may even be why your business is not getting qualified prospects regularly, not closing sales consistently. You lack the revenues and profits you want and need.

Hiring the right small business marketing consultant will not only improve on your current marketing, but the consultant will also help you overcome your biggest business challenges, too. They will understand your challenges, and they will know how to solve them. Additionally, the small business marketing consultant will have a tool kit of proven marketing strategies and tactics to move your business in the right direction. If you are not an accountant or an attorney, you do not pretend to be one and do their work, right? The same with marketing. Marketing is constantly changing. It would be nearly impossible for you to have the knowledge and expertise a dedicated marketing professional has. Be the expert in what you are brilliant at and hire a marketer.

You do not have a conveyor belt of qualified "A" prospects.

The biggest issue I see—and why so many small businesses fail—is that they lack qualified prospects coming to them. They are not using the Conversion Equation and do not understand how to do reverse marketing. They spend all their time hunting for prospects and meeting with many unqualified prospects. Without enough "A" prospects continually being generated for your business, it is impossible for your business to thrive fully and reach its potential. A small business marketing consultant will help you identify why you are not getting enough prospects and why your prospects are not mostly "A" prospects. They will apply the Conversion Equation and customize it for you so your business can start swimming in leads.

Prospects are not converting into enough sales.

Not converting prospects into sales can be caused by many things. Often the prospects being generated for the business are not "A" prospects. Sometimes the business may have a difficult time converting "A" prospects to buyers. The business might lack a sales and conversion process designed with the right powerful questions. A marketing professional will look at all of your business processes. They will then identify where things are breaking down in your marketing, and they will create the strategies, tactics, and a customized plan to fix what is not working in your business. Many times, businesses have prospects but not the right "A" prospects. Sometimes a business does not need to generate more prospects; they simply need to convert more of the leads they already receive! A small business marketing consultant will do a deep dive into your understanding of your current prospect generation and closing and conversion processes.

Lack of focus.

I always tell my client family members, "one focus, one goal." I find that most small business owners are wearing a lot of different hats. They are doing everything in their business from accounting, social media marketing, online and offline marketing, podcasting, blogging, article writing, creating content, doing human resource tasks, etc. Their personal lives and free time and freedom are suffering as a result of this. Their business has simply become another job for little pay and long hours. Their personal lives, health, and wellness are being sacrificed because of their business. As a business owner, there are so many tasks that you must complete. Marketing is the most important task for the health and wealth of your business. You must be working on your marketing daily and committed to with your full focus and attention. This is where a professional marketing consultant comes in. They will ensure you can focus on the other important parts of your business, and you will know with confidence your marketing is on the right track every day.

You are a cookie-cutter business.

If your business looks or sounds like your competitors, you will only have one thing ever to differentiate you: price. That is a losing battle. A small business marketing consultant will help you implement a customized, proven, solid marketing strategy that will allow you to define your difference clearly and why customers should buy from you. This CUPS will have you stand alone in the marketplace with no jargon, and you will no longer be an apples-to-apples business. You will be able to charge higher fees as your products and services will provide greater value to your customers.

CHAPTER 17
HERE TO HELP YOU!

I wrote this book because I love helping business owners just like you. Like me, you have a desire to serve others and make a difference with your products and services. I know I am speaking to the Heart-repreneur® part of you who stands for integrity, authenticity, and transparency. I want to help you with my proven and guaranteed 200% return on investment marketing. My approach is unlike any other small business marketing consultant. I help you create and sustain your business growth and marketing success, without increasing advertising costs!

Not only am I a Master Certified Guerilla Marketing Trainer and Coach, but I am a licensed Hidden Marketing Assets Business Consultant. I hold a Ph.D. in organizational behavior and clinical psychology. I have created *8* different multi-million-dollar business of my own. I have helped over 6,000 businesses like yours to become six-, seven-, and some even eight-figure business in over 400 different industries. I am a best-selling author of over 40 titles on business, sales, and marketing. I am a keynote speaker worldwide on these topics, and I host a popular radio show, podcast, blog, and TV show dedicated to helping small business owners like YOU! I have been myopic for over 40 years on business growth! No one provides my guarantee—200% return on investment, or I give you all your money back and write you a $5,000 check if I fail.

If you and I decide to work together, I will first look at your current marketing assets. I am truly an expert at identifying the wealth of hidden marketing assets in your business. I will help to identify and optimize these assets in ways that will potentially give you dramatic growth increases quickly. Typically, I can help an established business grow from 25% 100% in only about 3-6months. And I do this without your business having to invest a lot of money into marketing and advertising—and without a lot of costly or time-consuming changes in your business.

Today, the marketplace is highly competitive for all small businesses. Having solid, proven marketing systems in place is vital to your business's long-term success. My marketing consulting is unique due to my ability to leverage and optimize the marketing assets that already exist within your business. This approach to marketing is foreign to most small business marketing consultants. My guaranteed approach will lead to newfound sources of revenue and profit for your business.

Let me explain why my small business marketing consulting will work in your business—and how I can make the bold claims I make and offer the guarantee I provide.

First, let me ask you some questions that will help me identify IF you are an "A" prospect for my company to help.

Do any of these currently exist in your business?
- Past customers
- Special knowledge or expertise
- Unique products or services
- Underperforming closing rates
- Marketing and advertising that does not get results
- Current customers
- Relationships with other businesses
- Average unit per sale amount
- Back-end products
- Community reputation
- Branding

- Prospective customers
- Website or great location
- Expertise
- Quality products and services
- Low closing and sales conversion ratios
- Competition
- Marketing efforts that do not work
- Packaging or bundling of products and services

If you said yes to anything on this list, you are a potential business that my company can help. We will begin by evaluating your marketing for the most common mistakes. Such as:

- You lack a CUPS and have not promoted your CUPS everywhere.
- You are running ineffective advertising.
- You are cutting prices on the front-end and have no back-end marketing plan.
- You are doing marketing that is not tested or where all marketing components are not being tested.
- You are not applying the Conversion Equation in all of your marketing.
- You do not know the 8 essential pillars of marketing.
- You lack strategic endorsement partners, affiliates, and joint venture partners.
- Your marketing messages *"tease and titillate"* instead of interrupting, engaging, educating and offering.
- You are using tactics in your marketing that have no proven effective strategy behind them.

Answer the above questions with total honesty. If any of these statements apply to your business, I can help you grow your business. Why?

The guaranteed effectiveness, the brilliance, and the power of Heart-repreneur®'s proprietary and proven marketing system is that it works three ways to grow any business without increasing advertising or marketing cost. Our marketing system will grow your business by:

- Attracting more customers
- Increasing your average sale
- Increasing your repeat purchases and closing ratios

When we integrate these three factors into your business, you can expect to see what our client family members see exponential business growth at a rate of 25% to 300%. Why?

This marketing system works without increased advertising or advertising costs in most cases, so the result is more profit for your business.

How can we achieve these results? We use 8 marketing pillars, while most small business marketing consultants only use a few. To me, that is like sitting on a three-legged chair and knowing the chair can collapse at any moment.

The 8 Marketing Pillars

These pillars that all your marketing must be based on so that you can organically achieve business growth. These eight pillars are the foundation of our marketing system and will increase your revenue and profit when installed correctly in your business while reducing your cost per qualified lead. Each of the steps that comprise the eight pillars is designed to be measurable and increase your revenue and profit consistently. Some of my client family members experience more success from one part of the system than another and that is to be expected.

As we work together to implement the system in your business, not only will you enjoy increased revenue and profit, your business will be built on multiple marketing pillars giving you greater marketing stability. You will also enjoy greater loyalty and responsiveness from your past and present customers. The eight pillars include a number of necessary processes and steps.

At Heartrepreneur LLC, I have put together a highly qualified and unique team of small business marketing consultants who specialize in the Conversion Equation, finding hidden marketing assets, and who will guide your business to have all of the eight pillars in place. We also keep your time investment minimal as we realize this is of importance for you and we want you to be enjoying your life, family, vacations, and free time, too!

We are the ONLY small business marketing firm that guarantees a potential 200% return on your investment. We not only refund all your money if we fail, we also write you a check for $5,000 for wasting your time. We guarantee your success.

Our client family members tell us that the investment they make in our marketing consulting services is more than completely paid from their increased revenue and the profits our system generates for them.

Here are the 8 foundational pillars that make up our complete and fully guaranteed marketing system.

Pillar 1: To uncover your niche, the results your niche desires, and to define and create your Core Unique Positioning Statement*

Pillar 2: To integrate your CUPS into all your marketing using the Conversion Equation

Pillar 3: To facilitate the creation of your database management and marketing including your drip campaigns

Pillar 4: To identify and grow your strategic alliances and your joint venture partners

Pillar 5: To identify the right media for your marketing messages and put this to work for your business

Pillar 6: To foster your company's brand recognition and identity—and position you and your company as the credible, reliable experts in your niche

Pillar 7: To assist with the creation of effective direct marketing campaigns

Pillar 8: To facilitate responses from your internet marketing including websites, opt-ins, blogging, social media posts, and engagements

Testing

Our small business marketing consulting is not a cookie-cutter. We help you generate prospects with personalized messaging and communications to have your products or services stand out and be noticed by your ideal target audience. Sure, you can get an email to land in your prospects in-box or you can send a piece of snail mail to a prospect's mailbox. That is not where the real marketing challenge is. The real challenge is to stand out from all of your competition by interrupting them, engaging them, educating them, and motivating a prospect to accept your offer and take action through reverse marketing.

Effective marketing is always done based on testing, tweaking, refining, measuring, and having an arsenal of no-and low-cost marketing strategies. We have over 300 proven tactics in our Guerilla Marketing toolkit.

We help you select the right marketing strategies, then we match the appropriate data with the right creative design and messaging that connects with your applicable consumers. We then choose the right tactics to implement for your business. As marketing professionals, we always test and fine-tune your marketing to ensure optimal results. We also use a mix of marketing vehicles both on and off-line, too.

Historically, database marketing relied overwhelmingly on direct mail. Then increasingly telemarketing has been used. And now, there are many alternatives to consider, including e-mail, social media, a website, etc. Particularly for closing sales for higher-ticket goods or services, a combination of several different contact methods may work best.

For example, you may first send a direct-mail piece to "warm-up" a prospect and then phone to get an appointment where you try to close the sale in person or by video conferencing. Or in a direct-mail piece, you may refer the prospect to a website or an email address where the prospect can get more information without hesitating because they do not want to talk to a salesperson just yet.

We rely on drip campaigns and email with many of our client family members because it is no cost and does not push people to have a meeting too quickly. Email is a great way to build and manage effective follow-up campaigns and connect with your prospects and current customers. I recommend email to all my client family members even if they need to build a database from scratch. Email is easy to track and to use for testing purposes as well. We already have templates of effective emails and can quickly make them applicable to your business.

Everything we provide with our small business marketing consulting is not only cost-effective, it is designed to be efficient. We utilize an integrated approach to growing and retaining your customer database. Our client family members find that our system is easily implemented in their businesses and serves to drive new qualified "A" customer leads while constantly strengthening their customer relationships.

A Look at Our Marketing and Business Consulting Services

If we accept you as one of our client family members, we will analyze your current marketing, advertising, and sales systems as well as define your overall business growth objectives.

- Who is your target audience?
- What are they looking for?
- What are their online and offline habits?
- What is your Core Unique Positioning Statement*?

From there, we work with you to create your customized marketing plans, your overall marketing strategy, and marketing actions. We help to create systems specifically tailored to your company's needs.

Heartrepreneur LLC provides strategic business and marketing consulting services that allow our client family members to leverage both marketing and technology to their benefit. Our consulting integrates technology and marketing, too. We have combined experience of over 100 years. We have worked with companies to refine their business and marketing plans, create new revenue streams, automate business processes and procedures, and better utilize cutting edge technology.

We are a full-service business, sales, and marketing company that diligently works to maintain our standing as the most advanced business and marketing company on the planet—while offering a full range of comprehensive marketing programs for every budget.

Integrated Marketing

Integrated marketing services or integrated marketing communications, weaves all of your marketing efforts into one cohesive marketing campaign.

Integrated marketing services include elements from brand and image development, advertising, and public relations to traditional marketing such as print, radio, and television advertising to non-traditional marketing such as internet marketing, search engine marketing, search engine optimization, and pay-per-click advertising.

Each element of your marketing is designed and integrated to further your companies' brand and message. Whether you are looking for a comprehensive marketing solution or a single marketing tool to engage your audiences, we can help you develop and implement customized, proven marketing strategies that work. They are aligned with the Conversion Equation, which is the backbone of everything we do. Our ability to consolidate and integrate these services into one comprehensive solution sets us apart from our competition. I have a team of highly trained integrated marketing consultants who will work with you to deliver your message across several forms of media, and you also have the opportunity to work directly with me, as our client family members do.

Interactive Marketing

We call the act, process, or technique of promoting, selling, and distributing a product or service interactive marketing. In order to continue to thrive, companies must acquire and retain customers. Marketing conveys your message consistently to your ideal prospects, helps you to discover what your customers want and need, what price they will pay and where to find the prospects that will most likely buy from your business.

Unfortunately, all too often, businesses do not have a solid plan, strategy, or system. They invest in the typical advertising such as pay-per-click, Facebook ads, even radio, and print ads just to throw it out there to see what sticks. Then they sit back and wait to see what happens. For what?

Without planning, research, tracking, and analysis, your marketing efforts will fail. Our interactive marketing approach consists of understanding your customer's needs, developing a marketing strategy, building and implementing an integrated marketing plan, and tracking the results. Although the process seems simple, most companies have a hard time developing an interactive marketing strategy that *interrupts, engages, educates,* and makes the right *offer* to their prospective audience.

How do you approach the process of marketing products and services?

To be effective, supporting elements, such as targeting and positioning, must be an integral part of your plan. A marketing strategy consists of a cohesive melding of whom you are targeting, positioning your business to differentiate yourself from your competitors and what features your product or service will have. It also addresses what message to send and how to send it, what price you will charge, and how you will respond to customer service.

Marketing can be a complicated and expensive venture, especially when it comes to on-line marketing. To be successful, it is important to partner with a marketing consulting company, which keeps up to date and knows the tricks of the trade. Most importantly, you must partner with a company you can trust and one that provides a solid track record with proven results and a guarantee where they take the risk because they are certain they can get your business results. Most of our client family members have been burnt in the past by our competitors—who have all claimed to be able to get them to more prospects, close more sales, and make more revenue and profits.

Why Heartrepreneur LLC Stands Alone

Our small business marketing consulting is unique in four ways, which I will share in a moment. Keep in mind everything we do is done specifically for each client family member. The system we design for you will optimize and redeploy all underutilized or overlooked marketing strengths within your company while simultaneously working the many different ways to grow your business. For qualifying companies, our consulting, our proprietary system, and its implementation is guaranteed to potentially generate a 200 % plus increase in revenue, or we are willing to return your entire investment plus write you a $5,000 check if we fail. We take all the risk because we know our consulting works.

If we accept your company as one of our client family members our marketing consulting will be your complete A to Z turn-key solution complete with marketing implementation in place and responsible for every aspect of the fulfillment effort.

Heartrepreneur LLC is unique in 4 ways

1. We look at marketing differently and we have a proven, systematic approach to growing your business.
2. We simultaneously grow your business in three ways and on eight marketing pillars.
3. We apply the Conversion Equation, so your business grows by reverse marketing.
4. We guarantee a 200% potential ROI in revenues, or we give you your money back plus we write you a check for $5,000 if we fail.

Our Unique Approach

We view marketing in a way that is different from most traditional approaches to marketing. We have a proven, and guaranteed system that seeks out and better employs your company's under-utilized, forgotten, or overlooked marketing strengths (hidden marketing assets). Such assets include your current marketing, sales, your and/or your employee or staff expertise, customer base (past, present, and/or prospective), business relationships and day-to-day policies and procedures, just to name a few. These assets become reclaimed, optimized, leveraged, and redeployed with our marketing consulting. This redeployment creates new streams of revenue and profit. Our proprietary marketing system is unique in that it not only creates—but also improves your marketing systems. It is in the implementation and performance of the system that this is guaranteed.

The Genius of the System

The genius of our proprietary marketing system is that as your hidden marketing assets are optimized—and as your multiple marketing pillars are developed and implemented—you will find that your business will grow in 3 ways:

1. Increase in prospects
2. Increase in the conversion rate of prospects to customers
3. Increase in the value or worth of each customer

Together, we will work at growing your business in these three ways. This is the key to achieving potential revenue growth of potentially 200%. We work on exponential growth, which means a little improvement in each area will have dramatic overall results to your bottom line.

Benefits of Using Our Proprietary System in Your Business

These are the results we typically get for our client family members.

1. More Customers: All elements of your marketing will tastefully, elegantly, and enthusiastically invite your prospects, customers, and clients to ONLY do business with you and your company.
2. Increased Revenues and Profits: Our system is so thorough and methodical you can use it over and over to create on-going streams of income. Our marketing consulting will uncover marketing assets and turn them into unexpected windfall profits for you.
3. Improved Productivity for You and Your Employees: We can transform you and your employees into highly effective, motivated, and profitable people. The system is so easy to understand and implement, you and your employees will finally have a step-by-step program to implement and make your company more profitable.
4. Efficient and Profitable Marketing: Heartrepreneur LLC operates by the standard of measurable results. You will know if any cost of marketing or advertising is worth the price. You will never waste a penny in useless, wasteful advertising.
5. Enjoyable Process: If you decide to apply to become one of our client family members, you will have us by your side. You will be headed for not only more profits, but also an enjoyable, educational, and empowering experience as well.

Getting Started

We begin with an upfront, diagnosis, and needs analysis consultation. You will meet with one of the top consultants on our team who is guaranteed to find your business money. If your business is a start-up, we will uncover $10,000 or more of hidden assets. If you are an established business, we will find $100,000 or more of hidden marketing assets. We guarantee this, and if we fail we will cheerfully refund your money—and you are going to invest less than $100 for this process which is valued at over $4000 because we will also send you an entire Blueprint that is customized for your business which you can implement with our without our help

During this meeting, we will begin the process of identifying your needs and identifying your hidden marketing strengths. The result of this meeting will be the creation of your customized marketing Blueprint by our marketing expert and will be specifically designed for your business. We will then help you to systematically implement the plan with a series of practical recommendations to start improving your company's sales and profits.

Schedule your session right now. (www.tlwebinar.com/blueprint)

We would love to talk to you and give you an idea about the many ways we can help you increase your marketing performance and profitability.

CONCLUSION
ONE LAST WORD OF ADVICE

U nlike most business coaches, marketing consultants, or others in the small business help industry, we are a results-based marketing consulting company that assists small to medium-sized businesses in creating and implementing comprehensive, proven and guaranteed marketing programs and systems. We empower business owners to meet the future's challenges through increased productivity and increased performance in their marketing. Our approach to growing your business is one that you simply will not find from your everyday marketing, advertising, sales coach, or consultant.

For many years, traditional marketing philosophy has been based on a theory researched and developed by large corporations. In practice, this philosophy is based on the assumption that investing large sums of money on expensive online and traditional advertising will bring in more new prospects for your business. Then, hopefully, the increase in prospective customers or clients will create the desired growth and offset ever-increasing expenses. Properly applied, this philosophy can work very well for a business with a large advertising budget. But what about your small to medium-sized companies? As evidenced by the shocking failure rate of small businesses today, this marketing philosophy is miserably outdated, if it ever worked.

So why do businesses keep doing it? It's simple. No one has shown them a better way from a different objective and more effective viewpoint, a viewpoint that makes every dollar you spend promoting your business is traceable, accountable, measurable, and comes back to you quickly and in multiples. It is a viewpoint that looks at all the many ways to grow a business and works those ways concurrently.

It is this approach to marketing that we and only we will give you. Our philosophy is revolutionary in its simplicity and is an approach that you simply will not find from your everyday marketing, advertising, business or sales coach or consultant and comes with an unparalleled, rock-solid guarantee. We guarantee a 200% potential return on your investment or we refund your money plus send you an additional check for $5,000 if we fail. No other marketing coach or consultant guarantees their work. We believe our compensation must come from actual results generated.

Heartrepreneur LLC concentrates on qualified segments and types of business as our potential client family members. We know that our techniques and ideas will work for most businesses in that group, but not all. This is why we provide the Profit Acceleration Session (www.tlwebinar.com/blueprint) finding your business money right away and why we also create and give you the actual customized Blueprint for your business.

If we believe we can help you, during this consultation and have identified your needs and we are confident you are a fit we will offer you the ability to become one of our valued client family members. If we accept you, you will commit to a weekly consulting session and to do the weekly homework, and we will commit to guaranteeing your success. This Profit Acceleration Session will determine whether our techniques will work for your particular business and is also fully guaranteed, or we give you the money back you invested. You still walk away with our consulting help and your customized marketing action Blueprint you can implement in your business.

I promise you that this session is advisory and not a sales pitch in disguise and will give you more clarity. During the session, we will help you understand the right short and long-term targets your business must implement, the steps you need to take to achieve your targets, and how to measure your marketing's success. Together we will develop absolute clarity about where you are now and where you are going, what you want to achieve, the strengths and weaknesses of your business, and uncover the opportunities and threats that lie ahead.

We customize your marketing Blueprint and develop your plan and deliberately choose the right set of activities, tactics, and action methods. Here we bridge the gap between where your business is now, where you want your business to go, and decide the best ways to get your business there. We will identify which marketing tools are required, what skills you may need, and gather information needed to decide if we can successfully implement our business methods.

Implementation and Measurement

Have you ever heard the adage, "plan your work and work your plan"? I am not certain who said it, I just know that I fully resonate with it as a small business marketing consultant. Yet unimplemented ideas are still one of the biggest challenges small businesses face today. The entire reason we provide small business marketing consulting is that most small businesses have "failure to implement syndrome." They need someone by their side who is a trusted advisor and who will systematically help them by effectively and efficiently coordinating all of their marketing activities.

We deal with potential distractions, procrastination, and incorporate clear lines of responsibility into our consulting. At the end of the day how do you know if you have been successful? Measurement is a critical element in marketing.

Our program is based on clear, measurable, time-bound, and prioritized results. This is achieved by establishing and incorporating precise measurements of success and accountability into our marketing consulting. By measuring, we can analyze what results you are getting from your actions. We can then work at enhancing what is working and adjusting and fine-tuning the things that may not be working and we would like.

As different results are achieved throughout your marketing consulting and as successful ways to accomplish tasks are perfected, the focus of our consulting shifts to establishing various systematic processes in your business. This will be realized in improved performance, efficiencies, and successful automation, thereby transforming your company and your personal role into an efficient system that produces predictable results while saving you time and money.

We work with a limited number of client family members at one time. We only accept the businesses we know we can potentially get a 200% return on investment for as we are on the hook for a very bold guarantee. If you are accepted, this means you are a business that we know will make gains from our expertise, guidance, and support. Our consulting will be tailored to fit your needs, level of background, and type of industry. If you and your company qualify, after your Profit Acceleration Session and customized Blueprint, and if you want our help, we will begin your marketing consulting with our full diagnostic and our road map, customized for your business. This will reveal your current sales and marketing condition(s) and what keeps you from moving forward faster, and what to do about it and exactly how to get it done.

You will have your step-by-step customized sales, marketing, and business-building plan to follow with our help and our team of marketing and business growth experts to provide clarity and direction and walk step-in-step with you achieving your goals. We also have built-in accountability, so you make better use of your time, money, and energy. Once you have a clear picture of your most important outcomes, you can stay focused, productive, motivated, and on track.

Our consulting team will help you overcome fears, resistance, procrastination, and other barriers that previously have affected your actions as we all have a background in clinical psychology and business, sales, and marketing consulting. We build in motivation to keep business development a consistent part of your weekly activities.

We provide access to my team and me Monday through Friday from 9 a.m. to 5 p.m. Eastern and answer all your pressing "can't wait until the next business consultation" questions between sessions with direct "hotline" access to us. This is how we accelerate improvement and growth in your business. In every session, we are by your side, creating new standards of performance and excellence in visioning, planning, implementation and success, and assure efficiency in managing yourself and your time.

As your business increases from your sales and profit-building skills we share more advanced marketing and business-building techniques and strategies with you. If you have team members you want to involve in your consultations, we happily invite them to the sessions at no extra charge.

You and your team will have the timely and applicable insights, tools, resources, and ongoing support to move your business to the next level. And we will give you full access to our educational business academy (www. theultimatebusinessgrowthsystem.com), and "done-for-you" resource library of sales and marketing letters, scripts, templates, reports and systems for building your business. You will also have access to video training and weekly webinars with an expert from our academy to have all your questions answered.

By now, you hopefully can see the value the Conversion Equation will bring to your business if applied correctly. Do not go it alone. To our knowledge, we are the only small business marketing consulting firm that provides you with this performance promise and guarantee. As the saying goes, *"put our money where our mouth is"* and we do just that. You have no risk, nothing to lose and everything to gain.

Apply now. (www.tlwebinar.com/blueprint)

DON'T TAKE OUR WORD

Here's what others are saying about Heartrepreneur LLC.

Watch our client family members and hear what they say (www.theshortestwebinar.com)!

Here are just a few written excepts about our system performance as well.

Testimonials

Medical Office: "We had been running this one ad for three months, at a cost of $500 per run, and an average return of only $75. With your help and against the newspaper salesman's advice, we followed your advice and rewrote the ad and ran it for 3 days. I can't believe what a huge difference it made. The results were out of this world. I got 90 calls my first day and over 320 calls over the total three. From that ad, I gained 179 new patients and made over $53,000 in the first month. I continued to run it for 6 months and made over $400,000 that year from it."

—*Dr. LaJeanne Duke*

Chiropractor: "We were in debt $90,000 and had filed Chapter 11. Through utilizing concepts like joint venturing, we quickly grew our practice to 70-80 patients a day. We satisfied our debts, while cutting our advertising budget by $30,000 a year and getting out-of-town hospitals to fund most of our building."

—Family Health Centers

Dental Consultants: "Since we've implemented these marketing strategies, we have been able to grow by leaps and bounds. Our marketing has never been simpler or more systematic, and we increased our personal incomes by over $200,000 in one year."

—Cameron Consulting

University Professor & Performing Arts Theater: "Your methods are INCREDIBLE…I thank you for our initial session I put the things we talked about to work IMMEDIATELY and man, your input helped reframe my understanding and confidence in marketing overall. In the past, it was VERY frustrating as a Christian business owner to feel like other marketing groups didn't get my mission/vision. However, thanks to you and a couple of cups of Joe and a few hours at Starbucks, I am back on track. Can't wait to get more— and the book is on my shelf already so, one sold when you're done. Continued success and KEEP CREATING!"

—Vondell Richmond, NJ

Finance Company (Auto's): "Your consulting has been responsible for helping us to understand our unique position in the marketplace. The expertise in leadership, sales management, telemarketing, advertising, and direct mail all played key roles in our company's fast growth. We went from $1 million the first year, to $3.7 million the second, to over $5 million the third!"

—Jeff Savage

Mortgage Loan Broker: "These concepts and techniques are so unique and simple that you'll be amazed at how easy they are to grasp. I had a 100% increase in business from just one idea!"

—John Mallet, Citibank

Seminar Promotion Company: "We have been marketing seminars for many years now. Never once have we really tested the headlines on the letters we send out. We experimented and by flipping through the headline bank you gave us; we came up with a couple we thought were more powerful. Did it work? Did it ever! The next time we mailed, we went from a 2% response to over 4.5% response. This will mean an excess of half a million dollars in profits for us this year alone."

—*Darrel Bracken, Business Seminars, Inc.*

Auto Repair: "Your consulting helped me uncover and implement marketing ideas that increased our auto repair company's business 20% in three months. We started inviting our old customers back for more business and a small joint venture deal with a car dealer proved very effective. The marketing system you shared is different from other marketing plans in that his ideas cost very little to implement."

—*The Auto Shop*

Catering Company: "I implemented just a couple of ideas from our marketing consulting into my business, and in one year, I went from $350,000 to $500,000."

—*Howard Nelson, Fawn Whitney Catering*

Clothier: "These concepts are sound. The marketing techniques, coupled with great sales training, doubled our store's average sale from $25 to $50. And our customers come back regularly and buy from us more often. Sales have increased from $500,000 to over $750,000 in just 12 months."

—*Duane Jones, Owner, Cedar Creek Clothing*

Computer Hardware: "It's this simple. Before we hired you, we were doing $1,000 a week in new computer sales. Now we're doing $8,000 a week."

—*Molineux*

Health Program: "I consider myself to be a very astute businessman and marketer. It's very difficult to take anyone's suggestions, especially when I'm doing over $30,000 per month from my basement. But I was convinced to try a small change in my marketing. We went from $36,000 per month to over $68,000 the next month by making one little adjustment in our sales process. Wow!"

—*Dr. Samuel West, International Academy of Lymphology*

Magazine Publisher: "I was 27, had two kids, and no job, and my wife was pregnant. I needed an income badly. By using the concepts, I learned from you, I was able to create a direct mail offer by advertising in the magazine as a joint venture with a local newspaper. I quickly sold all of the spots to local health-related businesses and WHAM! My magazine was out on the street in full color, all 40,000 of them, and I had a $3,000 per month income."

—*Gordon Jacoby, Health & Fitness Guide*

Manufacturer: "Our business was suffering. I was about to file bankruptcy. Through reactivating my past customers, I created $10,000 in orders in one week and consistently $1,000 a day after that without any expenses whatsoever. Thank God!"

—*J.D. Seardall*

Moving and Storage: "Our conversion rate of prospects to customers increased 20%. This increase went right to our bottom line, as there was no increase in advertising expense."

—Owner, Global Van Lines Franchise

Office Supply: "We started just as an afterthought. By learning how to write an effective sales letter, we'll grow past $2 million in less than 2 years. We have learned how to grow a multi-million-dollar business."

—*Rich Harshaw, BTI*

Pizza Business: "In one fell swoop; I was able to almost eliminate Domino's and Pizza Hut from their advertising. It was ruthless, but it was them or me. These concepts have helped me expand my business to over 7 delivery areas without any more building space."

—Jim Casey, Jeno's Pizza

Radio Station: "I have used the techniques you taught me with phenomenal success. In fact, the last 25 clients that I have used your plan with have resulted in 24 annual contracts! We have also increased our average client worth by 300% and have turned clients who had been disappointed in solid accounts."

—Albert C. Gaige, Jr., WCVA/WCUl

Shoe Store: "Our average daily sales this time of year is about $1,200. By implementing just one idea you gave me my average day jumped immediately to $2,800 literally overnight."

—Owner, National Shoe

ABOUT THE AUTHOR

Terri Levine, Ph.D., is a business strategist and the Chief Heart-repreneur® at Heartrepreneur.com. She is a best-selling author, keynote speaker, radio and TV host, and appears regularly in the media as a business growth consulting expert. Dr. Levine has created her own successful businesses and has over 40 years of business, sales, and marketing experience. She has helped clients in 444 different industries and 19 countries and has worked with over 6,000 clients to date. Her methods are proven and guaranteed, as well.

Using the material in *Conversion Equation*, she grows service-based businesses to record levels while giving the owners more free time *and* increased income without having them feel like they need to be marketing experts or invest money in advertising.